PAT BROWN, MBA

Financial Literacy For Dentists

"Your Financial Playbook from Dental School to Retirement"

ABRAM 47 BROWN

First published by AbramBrown47 2025

First edition

ISBN: 978-1-967737-18-5

This book was professionally typeset on Reedsy.
Find out more at reedsy.com

Contents

Author's Preface

Financial Literacy For Dentists

Dentistry is a calling. It's a profession that demands technical precision, emotional intelligence, and years of rigorous education and sacrifice. But for all that training, there's one crucial subject rarely taught in dental school, residency, or CE courses: financial literacy.

I've had the privilege of working with professionals across many industries, but there's something unique about dentists. You're not just clinicians—you're often business owners, employers, real estate investors, community leaders, and primary breadwinners for your families. You walk into the operatory each day with skill and confidence, yet many leave their finances up to chance, overwhelm, or the default settings of an industry that doesn't always put your long-term interests first.

This book was born out of conversations—late-night emails from dental clients worried about student loans or practice overhead, lunch meetings filled with talk about retirement timelines, and hard moments of transition when life takes a turn: divorce, illness, burnout, or selling a practice. I've watched some dentists build incredible wealth, and I've seen others who felt behind, despite working harder than most people could imagine. What I've learned is this: the difference isn't intelligence. It's access to the right financial knowledge, at the right time, in the right language.

Financial Literacy For Dentists is that language. This book is your blueprint—whether you're a dental student still figuring it all out, an associate growing into ownership, or a seasoned practice owner looking toward exit strategy and legacy. You'll find practical guidance here on everything from budgeting and student loan repayment to practice valuation, retirement planning, investing, insurance, and estate strategy.

But more than that, you'll find a mindset shift. One that empowers you to see your money not just as something to manage—but as something to grow, protect, and align with your values.

I wrote this to help you take control of your finances so you can practice with freedom, live with confidence, and lead your family and your future with clarity.

Let's get started.

– Patrick Brown, MBA

Author, Financial Educator, and Wealth Advisor

Why This Book Was Written

Financial Literacy For Dentists

Dentistry is one of the few professions that blends clinical expertise with entrepreneurial grit. As a dentist, you're often expected to be a healthcare provider, small business owner, HR manager, real estate negotiator, marketing strategist, retirement planner, and financial steward—often all at once. But here's the catch: almost no one teaches you how to do all of that.

In dental school, you learn how to perform complex procedures, manage infection control, and improve patient outcomes. What you don't learn—what's rarely even discussed—is how to read a profit and loss statement, how to pay off $500,000 in student loans strategically, how to protect your income if you get injured, or how to build a financial plan that allows you to retire with dignity and choice.

That silence is why this book was written.

Over the years, I've had the privilege of sitting across from dozens—if not hundreds—of dentists, all in different stages of life and practice. I've seen the full range: the dental student who just matched into a residency program and is staring down a mountain of debt; the associate who's trying to decide whether practice ownership is worth it; the practice owner juggling staff turnover, equipment upgrades, and burnout; and the dentist in their late 50s wondering if they'll ever really be able to slow down and enjoy the life they've worked so hard to build.

In all these conversations, one truth has stood out: **it's not that dentists don't care about money—it's that most were never given a framework to understand it.**

No one explained how to budget on an inconsistent income while starting a new practice. No one broke down how to compare disability insurance policies or vet a financial advisor who understands the seasonal nature of collections. No one told them that wealth-building isn't just about earning more—it's about being intentional, informed, and protected.

This book is here to fill that gap.

Financial Literacy For Dentists is not about being flashy or "crushing it" in the markets. It's not a get-rich-quick scheme. It's a step-by-step resource that combines financial education with real-world guidance. It's about learning how to build wealth on your terms—whether you're trying to buy your first home, expand your practice, plan for kids' college, prepare for a transition, or simply sleep better at night knowing your finances are under control.

I wrote this book because I've seen what happens when smart, high-earning professionals are left in the dark about their money. I've watched talented dentists delay retirement because they didn't have a plan. I've seen others buy practices they weren't financially ready for, take on burdensome loans, or fall prey to salespeople posing as financial advisors. And I've also seen the other side—the dentists who, once educated and equipped, took full control of their money and built lives of freedom, legacy, and impact.

You don't have to become a finance expert. But you do need to understand how the financial world works around you—and more importantly, how to make it work **for** you.

This book was written to guide you through the financial milestones of your dental career—from school to retirement, from associate to owner, from paycheck to purpose. It will walk you through everything from cash flow management, debt reduction, insurance planning, investing, practice valuation, and legacy planning—all with a focus on empowering you, not overwhelming you.

Your hands already change lives. It's time to make sure your finances reflect that same level of precision, care, and excellence.

Let's start building—intentionally, intelligently, and with your values leading the way.

– Patrick Brown, MBA

Financial Educator, Wealth Advisor, and Advocate for Professionals Who Serve Others

The Financial Literacy Gap in the Dental Community

Let's get real for a second.

Dentists are some of the most intelligent, hard-working professionals in the world. You spend years mastering the art and science of oral health. You spend even more years paying off student loans, building practices, managing staff, and making sure your patients walk out smiling. But here's the truth that doesn't get talked about nearly enough: far too many dentists are financially underprepared—not because they're careless or indifferent, but because the system never gave them the tools in the first place.

Financial literacy is the missing course in dental school.

It's the one subject that doesn't show up on a syllabus, doesn't come with a board exam, and doesn't offer continuing education credits. And yet, it has more impact on your peace of mind, your lifestyle, your family's future, and your long-term freedom than most of the clinical skills you spent years perfecting.

This chapter is about acknowledging that gap—not to make anyone feel ashamed, but to open a new chapter where you are no longer navigating money in the dark.

What Do We Mean by Financial Literacy?

Financial literacy isn't about knowing every tax loophole or memorizing every investment term. It's not about being able to pick the next hot stock or mastering the real estate market on weekends. It's about having a working understanding of how money flows through your life—how to earn it wisely, manage it efficiently, protect it carefully, and grow it intentionally.

It's about knowing:

- How to read a P&L statement
- When to refinance your loans
- What kind of insurance you actually need (and what's just fluff)
- How to plan for retirement on your own terms
- How to prepare for the eventual sale of your practice
- How to protect yourself if you get sick, hurt, or sued
- How to say "no" to bad advice, sales pitches, and impulse decisions
- How to make money a tool, not a stressor

Financial literacy means having enough confidence in your money decisions that you don't have to second-guess yourself every time something financial comes up.

And for dentists, that confidence is often lacking—not because you're incapable of understanding money, but because you've never been taught how to.

Why Dentists Are Uniquely Vulnerable

Let's break it down. There are specific reasons why the dental community experiences financial literacy gaps at an even higher rate than other high-income professions.

1. You Start Behind—Way Behind

Most dentists come out of school with hundreds of thousands of dollars in student debt. Unlike some other professions where employers cover education or provide loan forgiveness, dentistry usually requires taking on that burden yourself. And unlike medical professionals who enter hospital systems or residency programs where income is slow and steady, dentists are often thrust into associate roles or entrepreneurial ventures with limited financial guidance.

You're starting life behind financially—at the same time your peers in other professions are starting families, buying homes, and investing.

2. You Don't Get Business Training—But You Need It

Dental school teaches you how to be a provider, not a CEO. But if you run or plan to run a practice, that's exactly what you are. You're managing overhead, payroll, lease agreements, vendor contracts, equipment financing, marketing budgets, and profitability targets. The business side of dentistry is overwhelming for many because they never received structured business education. You're expected to learn on the fly.

That's a dangerous position to be in—especially when your financial future depends on the long-term health of your business.

3. You're a High-Earning Target

Let's be honest: people see "D.D.S." or "D.M.D." and assume you're rich. The reality? High income doesn't always mean high wealth. But that perception puts dentists at higher risk of being sold expensive insurance policies, unnecessary financial products, and investments that serve someone else more than they serve you.

Without foundational financial literacy, it's hard to know what's useful and what's predatory.

4. You Have an Unpredictable Career Arc

The income journey for a dentist doesn't follow a straight line. Your early years are debt-heavy and income-light. Mid-career, you might hit your stride—but it depends on overhead, collections, patient flow, and how many chairs you're running. Later, you face declining energy, burnout, or physical limitations, and your practice may become more of a liability than an asset unless you've prepared to transition or sell.

All of this requires proactive financial planning. Without it, many dentists wake up in their late 50s and realize they've been sprinting on a treadmill that doesn't lead to a secure finish.

5. You're Time-Starved and Overwhelmed

The mental bandwidth it takes to run a successful practice, manage a family, keep up with continuing education, and maintain your personal health is enormous. For many dentists, financial planning gets pushed to the back burner—not because it's not important, but because there are simply too many fires to put out every day.

But just like oral health, financial health declines if it's ignored.

What the Gap Actually Looks Like

Let's put this in concrete terms. Here are just a few real-life examples of how this gap shows up in the lives of real dentists:

- Dentists who unknowingly purchase redundant or overpriced insurance policies they don't need
- Practice owners who don't separate personal and business expenses properly—and get burned come tax time
- Associates who never set up retirement accounts because "they'll do it later"
- Mid-career dentists who own successful practices but have little liquidity or emergency savings
- Professionals who trust the wrong advisor and lose hundreds of thousands of dollars in bad investments
- Dentists who delay estate planning, only for tragedy to leave their families in a legal and financial mess
- High-income earners who still feel broke because of lifestyle inflation, practice overhead, and poor tax planning

These aren't hypothetical. These are common.

And this is what makes financial literacy essential—not optional—for dentists.

Why This Isn't Taught (But Should Be)

So why isn't this being taught in dental schools or continuing education seminars?

Simple. Because it's not part of the traditional curriculum, and no one has taken ownership of this subject within the profession.

Dental schools are built to train clinicians—not business owners or investors. Even when business courses are offered, they tend to be broad, outdated, or more focused on how to open a practice than how to build wealth. Financial literacy is seen as something that should be outsourced to "your guy" (i.e., a financial advisor, accountant, or lawyer)—but when you don't know what to ask, how can you tell if you've found the right person?

This book argues: **You don't need to be an expert—but you do need to be literate.**

What Happens When the Gap Is Closed

When dentists develop financial literacy, everything changes.

- You become proactive instead of reactive
- You ask better questions
- You make decisions that align with your values and vision
- You say "no" to offers that don't serve you
- You sleep better at night
- You lead your practice with more confidence
- You start thinking long-term, not just "how do I survive this month?"

And perhaps most importantly: **you stop working just for money—and start making your money work for you.**

Bridging the Gap: What This Book Will Do

This book was created to close the gap. Not with theory, but with tools. Not with overwhelm, but with clarity. It walks with you, step by step, through the key financial decisions you'll face as a dental professional.

From the moment you graduate to the moment you retire, there are money moves to make—and landmines to avoid. This book breaks down:

- How to manage cash flow and budget realistically

- How to reduce student loan stress without wrecking your future
- What kind of insurance to get—and which types to skip
- When and how to start investing (even if you feel late)
- How to protect your practice as an asset—not just a job
- What to look for in a financial advisor, CPA, or attorney
- How to make estate planning part of your wealth-building—not just a box to check
- How to raise financially literate children in a high-income household
- And how to define success on your own terms—not someone else's

This book is not written to impress. It's written to empower.

Because once you have financial literacy, you don't need to fear money conversations anymore. You don't have to make decisions based on guesswork, pressure, or emotion. You move forward with purpose.

And when you combine that purpose with the drive and discipline you already have as a dentist? There's no limit to what you can build.

Closing the Gap, One Dentist at a Time

I've seen what happens when dentists don't get the financial guidance they need. I've seen careers stall, marriages suffer, wealth evaporate, and dreams delayed. But I've also seen what happens when financial literacy becomes part of a dentist's professional toolkit—when knowledge turns into clarity, and clarity turns into power.

That's why this book exists.

To close the gap.

To replace confusion with clarity.

To replace pressure with peace.

To replace burnout with balance.

And to help dentists not just practice dentistry—but live with confidence, security, and joy.

Let's close the gap—together.

Inspired by a Broader Mission

Financial Literacy For Dentists

This book isn't just about numbers. It's about people. It's about purpose. It's about the weight you carry as a professional who serves others all day—yet often carries the silent stress of money behind the scenes.

For most dentists, financial literacy isn't just about accumulating wealth. It's about freedom. It's about options. It's about creating the life you envisioned when you first decided to enter this field. You didn't spend all those years in school, clinicals, and practice building just to feel like a prisoner to your loans, your lifestyle, or your lack of a financial plan.

That's the deeper reason this book exists. It's inspired by a bigger mission—one that goes beyond dentistry, beyond balance sheets, and even beyond the dollars in your account.

It's about restoring control. About turning burnout into balance. About transforming confusion into confidence.

It's about making sure that the people who spend their lives caring for others are equipped to take care of themselves—financially, emotionally, and mentally.

I wrote this book because too many highly capable, deeply committed dental professionals feel behind when it comes to money—not because they're irresponsible, but because they were never taught how to think about wealth-building, risk management, or financial planning in a way that applies to their lives.

This mission started when I saw dentist after dentist—some in their prime earning years, others close to retirement—struggling to connect the dots. They had good income but lacked liquidity. They had beautiful homes but no estate plans. They had thriving practices but were exhausted and unsure how to exit. Many were trying to lead their teams, support their families, and keep the lights on at the office—but inside, they carried quiet financial anxiety that no one talks about.

And that's the part that hit me hardest—how quiet it is.

Because in your world, competence is assumed. Strength is expected. There's often little room to say, "I don't understand how this works" or "I'm worried I'm falling behind." Vulnerability, especially around money, can feel like weakness. But that silence is exactly what financial illiteracy feeds on.

My broader mission is to change that.

Not just with this book, but through a financial literacy movement that respects the complexity of your life, honors your profession, and speaks your language. Dentists don't need dumbed-down advice. You need frameworks, context, real-life examples, and trusted guidance tailored to your unique career path.

And this doesn't stop at you.

Because when you're financially confident, you model it for your team. You model it for your patients. You model it for your children. You pass it on—intentionally. You build not just a practice, but a legacy. You create the freedom to choose—whether that's scaling back, retiring early, giving generously, or finally taking the trip you keep putting off.

This book is one step in a much larger mission:

To help dentists claim agency over their financial lives.

To break generational cycles of financial anxiety.

To equip high-achieving professionals with tools they can use, not just advice they can't apply.

And to shift the culture—so financial empowerment becomes the norm, not the exception, in this profession.

If even one chapter of this book brings you clarity…

If even one section helps you make a decision with confidence…

If even one tool helps you teach someone else what you've learned…

Then the mission is already working.

And if you're ready to go from stressed to strategic—to stop reacting and start building—then you're part of that mission too.

The Goal

Financial Literacy For Dentists

The goal of this book is simple, but powerful: **to help you take control of your financial life—intentionally, confidently, and sustainably—through every stage of your dental career.**

Not just in theory. Not just with good intentions. But with real-world, practical guidance that you can apply whether you're still paying off student loans or preparing to sell your practice.

This book isn't here to turn you into a financial advisor. You don't need to memorize tax codes or master stock charts. What you do need is clarity. Structure. A plan that makes sense for where you are right now—and where you want to go.

Here's what this book aims to help you do:

- **Understand your finances in plain language**—so you don't feel like you're drowning in jargon, pressure, or conflicting advice.
- **Develop financial confidence**—so you can make decisions based on your goals, not your fears.
- **Avoid common traps** that dentists often fall into—like overbuying insurance, underfunding retirement, or assuming your practice is your entire net worth.
- **Learn how to build wealth that works for your lifestyle**—whether you're an associate, a practice owner, a specialist, or somewhere in between.
- **Create a personal roadmap** that aligns with your values, protects your peace of mind, and helps you build something you're proud to pass on.

The goal isn't perfection—it's progress.

You may not finish this book with every answer, but you will finish it with a new sense of awareness and direction. You'll know the right questions to ask. You'll have language for conversations with your financial team. You'll have a framework that puts you in the driver's seat—whether you're planning, protecting, investing, or rebuilding.

And most importantly, you'll realize that you're not alone. You're part of a growing community of dental professionals who are choosing to own their finances, rather than let their finances own them.

This book is your guide. But the real goal? **To make sure you never again feel behind, overwhelmed, or unprepared when it comes to your money.**

Part 1: The Dental School Years – Education, Debt, and First Paychecks

Part 1 of *Financial Literacy For Dentists* dives deep into the critical early years of every dentist's financial journey—dental school and the pivotal transition into earning real income. This section explores how the foundation of a dentist's financial future is often laid under the weight of student loans, clinical rotations, and long nights of study. It walks readers through the real cost of becoming a dentist—both financially and emotionally—and emphasizes the importance of developing financial habits early, even when the paycheck hasn't arrived yet.

We explore the mindset shift that must occur as students morph into professionals, discussing how to make informed decisions about borrowing, budgeting on a student's income, and preparing for the inevitable six-figure debt most will face. Then, we bridge the gap between graduation and that long-awaited first real paycheck, highlighting the emotional high of earning income and the financial low of realizing how quickly expenses—licensing, relocation, CE courses—can eat into it.

This section doesn't just talk about debt—it helps readers strategize around it. From choosing the right repayment plan to understanding deferment, consolidation, and forgiveness options, we provide actionable tools to take control instead of letting the loans control you. We also address how to navigate the first contract negotiations, avoid lifestyle creep, and make smart, foundational financial choices with that first real income.

By the end of Part 1, readers will walk away with a strong understanding of:

- How to frame their education as a long-term investment
- The true cost of dental school (beyond tuition)
- Smart ways to borrow, spend, and save during school
- The first steps to building a financial plan after graduation

This section sets the tone for the rest of the book—grounded, practical, and honest. It's about giving new dentists clarity, confidence, and a game plan for building wealth while doing the work they've spent years training for.

Chapter 1: Financial Survival in Dental School

Welcome to the Starting Line

Let's be honest: dental school is intense. The academic pressure, the clinical demands, the constant hum of expectations—none of that is light. But let's talk about the part that doesn't get discussed enough: the money.

Because whether you're sitting in your first week of classes or preparing for board exams, there's a good chance the cost of it all is sitting somewhere on your chest like a boulder. Tuition, fees, supplies, living expenses—and that's before we even talk about the interest on your loans. Financial stress in dental school is real. It's not just about numbers; it's about the way those numbers keep you up at night.

But here's the good news: you're not powerless in this. You're not stuck. You can build a financial survival plan that doesn't just help you make it through—but helps you start strong, with habits that'll serve you for the rest of your career. This chapter is about that plan.

The True Cost of Dental School

It's one thing to read the tuition on the website. It's another to see the full picture:

- Tuition and fees: $40,000–$100,000 per year, depending on your program
- Books, instruments, and supplies: $5,000–$10,000 annually

- Living expenses: $20,000–$40,000 per year
- Interest accumulation while in school: Thousands per year

Multiply that over four years, and many dental students graduate with $300,000–$500,000 in debt.

That's a mortgage—with no house.

But that's okay. Because the goal isn't to avoid debt altogether (for most, that's not possible). The goal is to manage it intentionally.

Step One: Face the Numbers, Don't Fear Them

If you don't know your numbers, you can't manage your money. Simple as that. Start by tracking:

- Your total student loan balance
- Your interest rates (Federal Direct Unsubsidized Loans, Grad PLUS Loans, private loans, etc.)
- Monthly interest accrual
- Your cost of living: rent, groceries, transportation, insurance, etc.

Action Step: Create a simple spreadsheet or use a free tool like Mint or YNAB (You Need A Budget) to start tracking.

Facing the numbers gives you clarity. And clarity gives you power.

Budgeting on a Student Lifestyle (Yes, It's Possible)

You're not making a full-time income yet—but you're likely spending like someone who is, thanks to loan disbursements. Don't let that fool you.

What to include in your budget:

- Housing (rent + utilities)
- Groceries and meals
- Transportation (car, gas, insurance, or public transit)
- Health and dental insurance (yes, even for you)
- Supplies and equipment
- Personal spending (coffee, clothes, entertainment)

Action Step: Set a weekly spending limit for discretionary expenses. Try $50–$75/week.

The Power of Saying No

You will be invited to dinners, weekend trips, and "you deserve it" splurges. But debt doesn't care about your social calendar.

It's okay to say no.

It's okay to choose lunch from home instead of takeout.

It's okay to skip the luxury scrub brand.

Your future self will thank you for it.

Understanding Student Loans While You're Still in School

Your loans are growing, even if you're not making payments. Let's break down a few basics:

- **Unsubsidized loans** start accruing interest immediately.
- **Grad PLUS loans** have higher interest rates and fees.
- **Private loans** may have less flexibility post-graduation.

Pros of Federal Loans: Income-driven repayment plans, loan forgiveness programs, deferment options.

Cons: High interest, can balloon quickly if unmanaged.

Action Step: If possible, make interest-only payments while in school. Even $25/month can save thousands.

Side Hustles: Should You Get One?

It depends on your bandwidth. Some students tutor, do freelance work, or even drive Uber.

Pros: Less reliance on loans, resume building, small sense of financial control.

Cons: Time tradeoff with studies, potential burnout, inconsistent income.

If you do it, treat it like a business: track expenses, set work hours, and keep school your top priority.

Avoiding Lifestyle Creep—Even Now

The more you get used to spending, the harder it will be to undo it later.

Dental students often fall into the trap of treating loan money like income. But it's not.

Create a standard of living now that you'd be proud to continue into residency or your first associate job. Remember, that car, that apartment, that vacation—it all comes with a price tag.

Scholarships, Grants, and "Found" Money

Most students assume there's nothing left to apply for once they start dental school. Not true.

Look for:

- Professional association scholarships (ADA, local dental societies)
- State-funded grants
- School-specific emergency funds or hardship grants
- Diversity and leadership scholarships

Action Step: Set a reminder to search and apply each semester.

Even $1,000 here and there makes a difference.

Mental Health and Financial Stress

Let's not sugarcoat it. Money stress affects everything—your sleep, your confidence, your relationships. Dental school already pushes you hard. Add financial anxiety, and it can feel unbearable.

You are not weak if you feel overwhelmed.

You are not behind if you haven't figured it all out.

Talk to someone. A mentor, a counselor, a financial coach. Getting support is smart—not shameful.

Long-Term Thinking in a Short-Term Season

Dental school is a season. A demanding one, but temporary. Every smart financial decision you make now will pay dividends—literally and figuratively—later.

Start thinking ahead:

- How much will your monthly payments be after graduation?
- What kind of lifestyle do you want to build?

- What financial habits do you want to take into your career?

Action Step: Write a one-page "vision statement" for your financial life after graduation. Be specific.

You Are Your Best Investment

It's easy to look at the loan balance and feel regret, fear, even resentment. But here's the truth:

You are your most valuable asset.

Your hands. Your mind. Your license.

You're training for a career that will give you the ability to help others—and earn income well into the six figures. That investment is real. But like all investments, it takes time to mature.

Trust the process. But also, be a good steward of it.

In Closing: This Is Just the Beginning

You don't have to have it all figured out today. You just need to take one small step toward clarity and control.

Face your numbers. Budget with honesty. Say no to debt-driven habits. Ask for help when you need it. And never forget: this season will end, and the future you're building is worth it.

You're not alone. You're not broken. You're becoming.

And you've got what it takes to make it—not just through dental school—but into a life of wealth, freedom, and purpose.

Chapter 2: Residency and Specialty Training – Paychecks vs. Pressure

When the Paycheck Starts But the Pressure Doesn't Stop

You made it through dental school. That alone is no small feat. And now, whether you're stepping into a general practice residency, an advanced education in general dentistry (AEGD), or a specialty program—welcome to the next chapter.

For many, this is the first time there's a real paycheck. Even if it's modest, it can feel like a relief after years of borrowing. But let's not sugarcoat it: this stage still brings its own set of financial pressures. Your income may barely keep up with your expenses, and your debt didn't magically disappear when you graduated.

In fact, for most dentists, this is the *tightrope season*—balancing between loan repayment, rising living costs, and the demands of training that often leave little time (or energy) to take full control of your financial life. This chapter is about walking that rope with clarity, courage, and a clear plan.

The Residency Paycheck: A Mixed Blessing

Most dental residency stipends fall between $40,000 and $60,000 a year. That's taxable income. And depending on where you live, the cost of living may eat up nearly all of it.

Let's break it down:

- **Monthly take-home (after taxes):** $2,500–$3,500
- **Estimated monthly expenses:**

- Rent: $1,200–$2,000
- Groceries: $300–$600
- Transportation: $200–$400
- Utilities & phone: $150–$300
- Loan interest (if you pay): $100–$300

There's not a lot left over.

Action Step: Build a "Residency Budget." Create categories for non-negotiables (housing, food, insurance) and limit flexible spending (entertainment, eating out). Use a budgeting app to stay consistent.

Do You Start Repaying Loans Now—or Wait?

This is one of the biggest financial decisions during residency. Here are the options:

Option 1: Deferment or Forbearance

- You won't have to make payments.
- But interest continues to accrue and capitalize.

Option 2: Income-Driven Repayment (IDR)

- Monthly payments are based on your income.
- May qualify you for Public Service Loan Forgiveness (PSLF) if your residency is at a non-profit hospital.
- Keeps you in repayment status without ballooning your balance.

Option 3: Pay Interest Only

- Keeps interest from capitalizing.
- Minimizes balance growth.

Pros of Paying During Residency:

- Lowers long-term debt burden

- Keeps you in good standing with lenders
- May qualify you for forgiveness programs

Cons:

- Reduces monthly cash flow
- Can feel overwhelming with a tight budget

Action Step: Call your loan servicer and get exact numbers. Then, run scenarios using the Federal Student Aid Loan Simulator.

Specialty Training: More Time, More Loans?

Pursuing orthodontics, oral surgery, endodontics, periodontics, or another specialty? You're likely looking at additional years of school—sometimes unpaid, sometimes with a small stipend, sometimes requiring more loans.

Questions to ask before pursuing a specialty:

- Will this increase my total loan burden?
- What is the average income in that specialty?
- What's the return on investment (ROI) of this path?

Example:

- Orthodontics may cost an additional $150,000 but lead to a starting salary of $250,000+.
- Pediatric dentistry may offer a quicker path to ownership with lower additional cost.

Action Step: Talk to three specialists in your desired field. Ask what they wish they'd known financially before choosing the path.

The Mental Load of Money in Residency

This season is emotionally complex. You're tired. You're working hard. You're trying to learn. And your bank account doesn't match the effort you're putting in.

Let's pause and name that:

It's okay to feel frustrated. It's okay to feel behind. It's okay to not have it all figured out.

But the key is not to give in to avoidance. When we avoid our finances, the stress grows. When we face them, even just a little at a time, the anxiety starts to shrink.

Marriage, Family, and Shared Finances

Some dentists go through residency while married or starting a family. This adds another layer of complexity—but also opportunity.

Tips for managing shared finances during residency:

- Communicate regularly about expenses and goals
- Use joint accounts for shared bills, but keep personal spending visible
- Agree on a "residency lifestyle" and stick to it

Pros: Potential dual income, emotional support **Cons:** Potential financial strain, child-care costs, one partner putting career on hold

Action Step: Create a shared financial calendar with key dates: paydays, loan due dates, rent, and goals.

Should You Moonlight?

Some residents can take on side work—especially in later years of residency or in programs that allow moonlighting.

Pros:

- Extra income to pay off loans or save
- More clinical experience

Cons:

- Time tradeoff
- Licensing limitations
- Malpractice coverage complexity

Action Step: Check your program's policy and your license status. If allowed, set boundaries. Don't let moonlighting burn you out.

Saving While Earning So Little: Is It Even Possible?

Yes, but it requires discipline and intention.

Where to start:

- Emergency fund: Aim for $1,000 to start
- Roth IRA: Contribute even $50/month if you can
- Use windfalls (tax refunds, gifts) to boost savings

The psychology here matters: Saving—even just a little—keeps you in the mindset of building, not just surviving.

Financial Tools and Habits to Start Now

Residency is the perfect time to lay the groundwork for future wealth.

What to do now:

- Track your spending
- Check your credit score
- Automate bills and payments
- Use free financial education tools (like podcasts, blogs, or webinars)

Why it matters: Financial confidence isn't about being rich—it's about being aware. Awareness leads to better choices. Better choices lead to financial freedom.

Planning for the First "Real" Paycheck

Residency doesn't last forever. Your attending years will come, and with them, a major income jump.

Start planning now:

- How much will you save from each paycheck?
- How quickly do you want to pay down loans?
- What's your timeline for buying a house or practice?

Avoid the trap of inflating your lifestyle just because your paycheck grows.

Action Step: Draft a post-residency budget. Dream a little. But plan first.

You Don't Have to Be Perfect—Just Present

Financial literacy in residency isn't about having the perfect spreadsheet. It's about awareness, small habits, and intentional steps. No one expects you to master everything right now.

But what you build during this time—financially, mentally, and emotionally—sets the tone for your future.

So show up.

Ask the questions.

Make the budget.

Say no when you need to.

Say yes to the life you're working so hard to build.

In Closing: Pressure Doesn't Have to Crush You

Residency is pressure-packed. There's no denying that. But it's also rich with opportunity.

Opportunity to build discipline. Opportunity to clarify what matters. Opportunity to get honest about money—and take ownership of it.

You're not behind. You're not alone. And you're more capable than you realize.

This season may feel long, but it's just a chapter.

Your story—of freedom, financial peace, and a career that empowers you to live fully—is still being written.

Chapter 3: Planning Ahead While Still in School

Why Thinking About the Future Isn't Premature—It's Strategic

Dental school feels all-consuming. You've got lectures, labs, patients, tests, boards, and what often feels like an endless stream of clinical hours. It can be hard to think beyond next week—let alone the next five years.

But here's the truth: your future starts now. Right now. Not when you graduate. Not when the loans come due. Not when you land that first associate job or residency. Today.

This chapter is not about creating pressure—it's about giving you permission to take control, plant seeds, and set the foundation for the financial life you *want*, not the one you end up in by default.

If dental school is the time to learn how to treat teeth, then let this chapter be the moment you learn how to treat your future.

The Case for Financial Planning as a Student

Let's talk mindset for a second.

A lot of dental students assume that because they're not making real money yet, they don't need to think about real financial planning. But that's exactly backward.

Here's why planning ahead matters:

- **You make hundreds of financial decisions during school.** (Housing, loans, credit cards, spending habits, insurance, etc.)

- **Habits form fast.** And financial habits formed in school are often carried into your career—for better or worse.
- **Your debt is growing.** But so is your potential. Managing one while nurturing the other requires a plan.

You don't have to have a six-figure income to make six-figure decisions.

Building a Vision Beyond Graduation

Planning ahead starts with asking: what kind of life do I want after dental school?

Some questions to ask yourself:

- Do I want to pursue a residency or go straight into practice?
- Where do I want to live?
- What lifestyle do I want to have in five years?
- Do I want to be an owner or an associate?
- How soon do I want to start saving for a house, travel, or retirement?

Write it out. Be specific. Even if it changes, you now have a target. And that target helps shape your financial choices *today*.

Action Step: Create a one-page "vision plan" that includes your short-term (1–3 years), mid-term (3–7 years), and long-term (10+ years) financial goals.

Loan Strategy 101: Start Managing Before You Graduate

Loan planning doesn't start when you start making payments. It starts the moment you take them out.

Understand your loan types:

- Federal Direct Unsubsidized Loans
- Federal Grad PLUS Loans
- Private Loans (if any)

Know these terms:

- Interest rate
- Capitalization
- Grace period
- Repayment plan options (IDR, REPAYE, PAYE, PSLF, Standard)

Action Step: Create a running log of every loan you take out—type, amount, interest rate, disbursement date.

Pros of knowing early:

- Less stress after graduation
- Easier to qualify for forgiveness programs
- Ability to project future payments and total cost

Cons of ignoring your loans:

- Massive interest accumulation
- Limited repayment options
- Avoidance breeds anxiety

This isn't about shame—it's about stewardship.

The Magic of Micro-Saving

Yes, you can save while in dental school—even if it's just $10 or $20 a month.

Here's what micro-saving teaches you:

- That you can live with a little less
- That saving is a habit, not a dollar amount
- That you're capable of building discipline now

Open a high-yield savings account. Set an automatic transfer for $5 a week.

Action Step: Start an "Opportunity Fund"—money for future goals like CE courses, relocation costs, or even starting a practice.

It's not about the amount. It's about the behavior.

Start Tracking Your Spending—Now

Every dollar you spend while in school is borrowed money. Read that again.

That $12 takeout? It's really $20 with interest over time.

Tracking tools that work for students:

- YNAB (You Need A Budget)
- Mint
- Good old spreadsheets

Action Step: Track your spending for 30 days. You'll be amazed where your money actually goes.

Pro tip: Create spending categories: Essentials, Discretionary, Academic, Savings, and "Stuff I Didn't Expect."

Build Your Credit Without Digging a Hole

Your credit score will matter when:

- You apply for a lease
- You buy a home
- You open a practice loan
- You apply for credit cards or refinance loans

Tips for building credit wisely:

- Get a student credit card with no annual fee
- Use it once a month for a small purchase (gas, groceries)
- Pay it off in full *every* month

Action Step: Check your credit score for free at annualcreditreport.com and set a calendar reminder to check it every four months.

Get Organized: Documents, Passwords, and Systems

Dental school is busy, but it's the perfect time to start building your financial system.

What you'll want to organize:

- Loan documents and contacts
- Insurance info
- Bank and credit accounts
- Tax documents (yes, even now)
- Scholarship and grant letters

Use a password manager. Back up your files. Create digital folders labeled by year.

Future you will be grateful.

Insurance 101 for Dental Students

Even in school, there are some insurances worth thinking about:

Health Insurance: You may be on your parents' plan (until 26), or need school coverage. **Renter's Insurance:** Protects your stuff for cheap. **Disability Insurance:** If you're injured and can't finish school or work, this could be a lifeline.

Action Step: Get quotes for long-term disability coverage with a future increase option—it's cheaper now and locks in your insurability.

Start Learning the Business of Dentistry—Now

Dental school doesn't teach business, but you can start learning:

- Read dental finance blogs and books
- Attend free webinars by dental CPAs or advisors
- Follow practice management content
- Talk to practice owners

Topics to look into:

- Overhead and profit margins
- Associate vs. ownership income
- Tax structure for dental practices (S-Corp, LLC, etc.)
- Lease vs. buy for equipment

Action Step: Set a goal to read one finance-related article per week and write down one takeaway.

Networking: Your Financial Secret Weapon

The people you meet now—classmates, instructors, mentors, alumni—will shape your financial life more than you realize.

Build real relationships. Ask questions. Stay curious.

Action Step: Create a contact list of mentors, advisors, financial professionals, and practice owners. Reach out with curiosity, not just career questions.

Think Like an Owner, Even if You're Not One Yet

Planning ahead means stepping into the identity of someone who's going to lead one day. Whether you're building a practice or running your household finances, think like the CEO of your life.

That means:

- Making proactive decisions, not reactive ones
- Seeking out education before it's "necessary"
- Protecting your time, energy, and money

Ownership mindset tip: Don't say "I'm just a student." Say, "I'm preparing to lead."

Reflection: You're Not Just Getting a Degree—You're Building a Life

Dental school is about becoming a dentist. But life after school is about becoming a steward of everything that comes with that title—your income, your debt, your impact.

Planning ahead doesn't make you uptight. It makes you free.

Free to make informed choices. Free to turn down opportunities that don't align. Free to build wealth and generosity instead of just trying to "catch up."

You're not behind. You're exactly where you need to be.

And the small steps you take now? They compound—just like interest.

So start small. Think big. Keep going.

The future you want isn't some far-off thing—it's being shaped right now, one smart decision at a time.

Chapter 4: Should You Buy a Practice or Stay an Associate?

The Crossroads Every Dentist Faces

After a few years of working as an associate—or even just out of dental school—you'll likely find yourself standing at a familiar fork in the road:

Should I stay an associate, or should I buy a practice?

This decision is one of the biggest you'll make in your professional life. It's not just about money. It's about time, control, risk, reward, lifestyle, leadership, and long-term vision.

There's no universal right answer—but there is a right answer for *you*. This chapter is here to help you find it.

What It Means to Be an Associate

An associate dentist is employed (or sometimes contracted) by a practice. You treat patients, follow the protocols set by the owner, and focus primarily on clinical work.

Pros:

- Predictable income
- Fewer administrative headaches
- Less financial risk
- Easier to balance life and work in early career
- Time to sharpen clinical skills and build speed

Cons:

- Limited control over patient flow, team, or equipment
- Often capped earning potential
- No equity or long-term stake in the practice's success
- Vulnerable to sudden changes in employment

Who this path is good for:

- New graduates still building confidence
- Dentists who want a better work-life balance
- People who don't enjoy business or leadership tasks

Action Step: Track your net income for 12 months. Compare this to what a practice owner in your area is taking home (not gross revenue, but actual income). Use that data in your decision-making.

What It Means to Buy a Practice

Practice ownership means you're in charge. You're the CEO, clinical lead, and financial strategist. Every decision comes through you.

Pros:

- Higher long-term income potential
- Full control over culture, systems, and patient experience
- Equity growth—your practice becomes an asset
- Ability to create passive income (through associates, hygiene department, etc.)

Cons:

- Large initial investment (loan or cash)
- Administrative responsibilities: HR, payroll, compliance, marketing, etc.
- More pressure and longer hours (at least initially)

- Financial risk if not managed well

Who this path is good for:

- Dentists who crave autonomy
- Those who want to build long-term wealth
- Leaders who enjoy building teams and systems
- People willing to invest time and energy for future payoff

Action Step: Create a mock budget. Include practice loan payments, payroll, overhead, and your desired take-home pay. This gives you a realistic preview of ownership.

How Much Does It Cost to Buy a Practice?

Typical acquisition prices range from **$400,000 to $1.2 million**, depending on:

- Location
- Annual collections
- Specialty
- Number of ops and staff

You'll likely need:

- 5%–10% down (often around $50K–$100K)
- Loan preapproval from a dental lender
- Solid credit and financial statements

Other startup costs include:

- Legal fees
- CPA/accounting setup
- Insurance
- Technology updates

- Marketing/rebranding

Action Step: Talk to a dental-specific lender. Learn how much you could be preapproved for *today*, and what you'd need to qualify for more.

What If You Want a Middle Ground?

There are options between full ownership and long-term employment:

1. **Buy-in partnerships:**

- Start as an associate, buy a percentage over time
- Pros: mentorship, shared risk
- Cons: slower path to control, potential conflicts

1. **Solo practice with associates later:**

- Start small, add team as you grow
- Pros: scalable, full control
- Cons: lonely early on, steep learning curve

1. **Corporate dental groups:**

- Can offer partial equity or leadership paths
- Pros: admin support
- Cons: less autonomy

Action Step: Interview three dentists who took different paths. Ask what worked, what didn't, and what they wish they'd known earlier.

Red Flags and Golden Signs

Red flags if you're considering buying:

- You're burned out clinically and think ownership will "fix" that
- You have no interest in leadership or managing people
- You're financially unstable (high personal debt, low savings)

- You've never reviewed or managed a budget

Golden signs you're ready to buy:

- You're excited by systems, team-building, and vision-casting
- You have clear financial goals and discipline
- You've observed a well-run practice up close
- You're emotionally ready to ride the ups and downs of ownership

How Long Should You Be an Associate Before Buying?

There's no magic number, but here's a guideline:

- **1–2 years:** Build speed, confidence, and exposure
- **3–5 years:** Ideal time to prepare, save, and assess ownership readiness

Too soon, and you may be unprepared. Wait too long, and you may leave wealth on the table.

Ownership Is Not Just a Job—It's a Lifestyle

Being a practice owner affects every part of your life. It can bring:

- Financial independence
- Flexibility
- Creativity and fulfillment
- Wealth through equity and real estate

But it also requires:

- Stress tolerance
- Constant learning
- Problem-solving
- Accountability for others' livelihoods

Ask yourself:

- What kind of life do I want?
- What's my risk tolerance?
- How do I define success?

In Closing: Know Your Why Before You Pick Your Path

Neither path is "better"—but one will be better for you.

Ownership isn't for everyone. But for those who want it—and prepare well—it can be the most powerful vehicle for freedom, purpose, and long-term wealth in dentistry.

Associateship isn't a fallback. It's a legitimate career choice that works beautifully for many dentists who want to focus on patient care without the burdens of business.

Clarity is the real win here.

So ask yourself, honestly and bravely:

What am I building? What matters most to me?

Then choose. Confidently.

Your path is yours to shape—and both roads can lead to success when taken with intention.

Chapter 5: The Business of Dentistry – Understanding Overhead, Profit, and Growth

Let's Talk Business—Because Dentistry *Is* One

You became a dentist to help people, to heal smiles, and maybe even to have some control over your schedule. But the moment you step into ownership—or even just entertain the idea—you're no longer just a healthcare provider. You're a business owner. And that changes everything.

If you're reading this as a new associate, this chapter is still for you. Understanding the numbers behind a practice—what it costs to run one, where the money goes, how profit is built—is not just for owners. It's for any dentist who wants financial clarity and control.

So let's break down what they *didn't* teach you in dental school.

Overhead: Where the Money Goes Before You Get Paid

Overhead is the total cost to run your practice. It's the money you spend just to keep the doors open. Understanding this is crucial—because it determines your profit, your salary, and your financial flexibility.

Typical Overhead Categories:

- Staff salaries and benefits
- Rent or mortgage
- Dental supplies and lab fees
- Equipment and tech maintenance

- Utilities and phone/internet
- Insurance (malpractice, liability, property)
- Marketing and advertising
- Loan payments (start-up or acquisition)

Average Overhead in Dentistry:

- General practice: 60%–75%
- Specialty practices: 50%–65%

If your collections are $1 million, and your overhead is 70%, that means $700,000 is spoken for. You're left with $300,000 for profit—and that includes your salary.

Action Step: If you're an owner, track your overhead monthly. If you're an associate, ask your employer about average overhead and what they prioritize.

Profit: What's Left After the Bills Are Paid

Profit isn't just your take-home pay. It's what's left *after* all expenses—including your own salary as a clinician.

In business terms, there's:

- **Gross Profit:** Revenue minus direct costs (like lab and supply fees)
- **Net Profit:** Revenue minus all costs (including rent, staff, marketing, etc.)

Healthy Net Profit Margins:

- 15%–25% is considered strong for a dental practice

Profit is not greed—it's sustainability. Profit allows you to:

- Reinvent the practice (new chairs, tech, training)
- Save for taxes and emergencies

- Pay yourself and your team well
- Take time off without financial panic

Action Step: Review your practice P&L (profit and loss) statement quarterly. Understand where the money flows and where you can tighten.

Collections vs. Production: Don't Confuse the Two

- **Production:** The work you've done (before adjustments)
- **Collections:** What you actually *get paid* for that work

Collections matter more.

High production with low collections = cash flow problems.

Typical Collection Rate Benchmarks:

- 96%–99% for fee-for-service
- 85%–90% for PPO-heavy practices

Action Step: Track collection rates monthly. Address issues like uncollected patient balances, denied insurance claims, or billing inefficiencies quickly.

Staffing: Your Biggest Asset and Expense

Staff costs can represent 25%–30% of your overhead.

And yet, your team is your practice. A great team = great patient experiences = repeat business and referrals.

How to manage staff costs without losing culture:

- Set clear roles and expectations
- Cross-train where possible
- Use bonuses tied to performance (collections, patient satisfaction)
- Invest in continuing education

Action Step: Review salaries annually. Benchmark them to local averages. Don't underpay—but be strategic.

Growth: What It Means and How to Pursue It

Growth isn't just about revenue. It's about sustainable expansion.

Types of Practice Growth:

1. **Patient volume growth** – more patients, more appointments
2. **Case acceptance growth** – improving how many treatment plans convert
3. **Production per visit** – maximizing each appointment's value
4. **Service expansion** – adding implants, ortho, or cosmetic procedures
5. **Location expansion** – second office or acquisition

Pros of Growth:

- More revenue
- Increased valuation (if you sell)
- Greater team opportunities

Cons:

- Higher overhead
- More complexity
- Greater leadership demands

Action Step: Define what growth *means* to you. Not everyone wants multiple locations. Choose your growth strategy wisely.

Marketing: You Need It—Even If You Hate It

Most dentists shy away from marketing. But if people don't know you exist, they can't become patients.

Smart Marketing Options:

- Google and Yelp review strategy
- Local SEO and website optimization
- Internal referral programs

- Community sponsorships
- Social media (authentic, not forced)

Action Step: Set a marketing budget (3%–5% of revenue) and measure ROI. Don't "hope"—test and track.

Technology and Equipment: Spend Wisely

Tech can streamline, impress, and increase production—but it's expensive.

Before you buy:

- Does it solve a problem or just look cool?
- Will it pay for itself in 12–24 months?
- Do you and your team know how to use it well?

Examples:

- CAD/CAM = faster crowns, fewer appointments
- CBCT = higher diagnostic value for implants, ortho

Action Step: Create an "equipment investment scorecard." Make purchases intentional, not impulsive.

The CEO Mindset: Becoming the Leader Your Practice Needs

Running a practice isn't just about teeth. It's about:

- Setting culture
- Making hiring and firing decisions
- Understanding taxes
- Reading P&Ls and balance sheets
- Managing burnout—yours and your team's

You're not just a provider. You're the CEO. The visionary. The strategist.

Action Step: Dedicate 1–2 hours a week to "business time." No drills. Just reviewing the numbers, setting goals, and planning.

Real Scenario: Dr. Moore's Growth Trap

Dr. Moore bought a growing practice. She increased marketing spend, hired two more assistants, and added evening hours.

Revenue increased. But her profit *dropped.* Why?

- Her collections lagged behind production
- Staff overtime wasn't budgeted
- Overhead ballooned before profit caught up

Takeaway: Growth must be strategic—not reactive.

Real Scenario: Dr. Shah's Lean Success

Dr. Shah kept a small solo practice with three ops and a tightly knit team. He focused on:

- Maximizing treatment acceptance
- Reducing no-shows
- Controlling supply costs

He netted 30% on $850,000 in collections—and took Fridays off.

Takeaway: Bigger isn't always better. Efficient and intentional wins the game.

In Closing: You *Can* Be a Great Clinician and a Great Businessperson

You don't have to choose. You don't have to become a shark to be successful. But you *do* have to pay attention.

Overhead, profit, and growth are not abstract ideas. They're the heartbeat of your financial life as a dentist.

And whether you're an associate dreaming of ownership or a seasoned owner trying to get your evenings back—know this:

You're capable of mastering the business of dentistry. You can learn the numbers. You can lead your team. You can grow—on your terms.

The chair may be your stage. But the business is your engine.

And now, you've got the keys.

Chapter 6: Building a Strong Financial Foundation Early

Let's start with a simple truth: the earlier you build a strong financial foundation, the better. That doesn't mean you have to get everything perfect out of the gate. But it does mean that the habits, systems, and mindset you establish in the early years of your dental career will shape the way money moves in your life for decades to come.

And whether you're fresh out of dental school, buying into your first practice, or looking up from a pile of debt and wondering what's next, this chapter is for you. This is where we slow it all down, clear the noise, and get back to basics.

You don't need a finance degree. You don't need to be perfect. You just need a game plan—and the willingness to take small, smart steps forward.

Start Where You Are

Let's clear something up right away: It's never too early—and never too late—to start building your financial foundation.

You might be:

- 28 years old, single, with six figures of student loan debt and no idea what a 401(k) really is
- 36, married with kids, running a practice, and feeling behind on retirement savings
- 42 and finally earning well, but still playing catch-up from years of financial triage

Wherever you are, the goal is the same: clarity, control, and a path forward. No shame. No comparison. Just progress.

The Cornerstones of a Strong Financial Foundation

There are five key areas that make up a strong financial foundation:

1. Budgeting and Cash Flow Awareness
2. Emergency Savings
3. Debt Management
4. Insurance Protection
5. Beginning to Invest

Let's walk through each one, the way I would if we were talking at your kitchen table or on your lunch break in the staff room.

1. Budgeting and Cash Flow Awareness

Let's start with the B-word. Most people hate the word "budget." It sounds restrictive, like something designed to make you feel guilty. But here's how I want you to think about it:

A budget isn't a punishment. It's a reflection of your values.

It's a way to tell your money where to go—before it disappears.

If you're a dentist, especially if you own a practice, you know the importance of cash flow. Think of your personal budget like your practice's operating system. You need to know what's coming in, what's going out, and where the leaks are.

Start simple:

- What's your total take-home pay each month (after taxes and withholdings)?
- What are your fixed expenses (rent/mortgage, student loan minimums, car payment, childcare)?
- What are your variable expenses (groceries, dining, travel, subscriptions)?

- Are you spending more than you're making?

Track your spending for 30 days—just once. You don't need to do it forever. But that one month will open your eyes.

Action Step: Use a spreadsheet, app, or old-school notebook to track every dollar you spend for 30 days. At the end, ask: Does this reflect who I want to be financially?

1. Emergency Savings

Before we talk about investing or buying into a practice, we need to talk about buffers.

An emergency fund is not a luxury—it's a necessity.

Life is unpredictable. HVAC systems break. Kids get sick. Associates leave your practice. You need to be ready.

For most dentists, a good goal is to have 3–6 months of personal living expenses saved in a separate, liquid savings account.

If you're a practice owner, you should also consider having 1–3 months of business overhead saved.

Pros of Emergency Funds:

- Reduces stress during unexpected events
- Prevents you from going into debt when life throws a curveball
- Buys you time to make smart decisions during a crisis

Cons (or better said, trade-offs):

- Money in savings earns little interest
- May feel like "idle" cash

But that's okay. This money isn't supposed to grow. It's supposed to protect.

Action Step: Set a goal to save $1,000 fast, then build to one month of expenses, then to three months. Automate it. Treat it like a bill.

1. Debt Management

Let's talk about the elephant in the room: student loans.

Most dentists graduate with six-figure debt. You're not alone.

But here's the thing—student loan debt is not a moral failing. It's a financial tool you used to earn a high-paying, respected profession. Now it's about managing it wisely.

There are multiple approaches:

- **Aggressive payoff** (focus on paying it down quickly)
- **Income-driven repayment** (pay based on what you earn)
- **Forgiveness plans** (for some public service or academic dentists)
- **Refinancing** (if you can lock in lower interest rates)

What's right for you depends on your goals, income, other debts, and whether you plan to buy a practice or a home soon.

Pros of aggressive payoff:

- Lower total interest paid
- Freedom and peace of mind

Cons:

- May delay investing
- Less flexibility

Action Step: Know exactly how much you owe, what your interest rates are, and what your minimum payments are. Run the math on your payoff options. Then choose a plan—and stick to it for a year.

1. Insurance Protection

Insurance isn't sexy. But it's necessary.

You've invested hundreds of thousands into your career. One accident, illness, or lawsuit could jeopardize everything.

There are four types of insurance every dentist needs:

1. **Disability Insurance** – Protects your income if you can't work
2. **Life Insurance** – Protects your family if you pass away unexpectedly
3. **Malpractice Insurance** – Shields you professionally
4. **Umbrella Insurance** – Extra liability protection

If you own a practice, you also need:

- Business overhead insurance
- Property and liability coverage

Action Step: Review your insurance coverage once a year. Don't just let it auto-renew. Get quotes, compare policies, and make sure your coverage matches your life stage.

1. Beginning to Invest

Now we get to the fun part: growing wealth.

Investing is how you turn income into long-term financial freedom. It's how you stop trading time for money.

But don't get fancy right away. Start with the basics:

- Max out a Roth IRA or Traditional IRA
- Contribute to a 401(k), SIMPLE IRA, or solo 401(k) if self-employed
- Set up a brokerage account for taxable investing

Compound interest is your ally. Even small amounts grow over time.

Example: Investing $500/month at 7% annual return for 30 years = over $600,000

Action Step: If you haven't started investing yet, set up a Roth IRA today.

Automate monthly contributions—even $100/month makes a difference.

What About Practice Ownership?

Buying into or starting a practice can be one of the most profitable financial moves you make.

But only if your foundation is solid.

Make sure you have:

- Personal emergency fund in place
- Clear understanding of your current debt
- Strong credit
- Good tax planning support
- A team of advisors (CPA, attorney, banker, insurance broker)

Pros of ownership:

- Higher income potential
- More autonomy
- Equity in a business

Cons:

- Financial risk
- Time and stress
- Requires upfront capital

Action Step: If practice ownership is on your radar, start having conversations now. Learn from other owners. Build your advisory team before you sign anything.

Taxes and the Dental Professional

The more you earn, the more taxes matter.

A good CPA is not optional. You need someone who understands dental practices, retirement accounts, business deductions, and how to minimize your tax burden legally.

Tax Tips:

- Track deductible expenses (CE, uniforms, travel, equipment)
- Maximize retirement plan contributions
- Use an S-corp structure if appropriate

Action Step: Schedule a tax planning meeting in Q3—not just in April. Be proactive, not reactive.

Closing Thoughts: The Power of Starting Strong

A strong financial foundation isn't about having everything figured out. It's about creating habits and systems that support the life you want to build.

It's about:

- Spending with intention
- Saving with purpose
- Investing with consistency
- Protecting your income and assets

And more than anything—it's about giving yourself room to grow.

You don't have to do it all today. Just take the next right step. Then the next. Then the next.

And remember: you're not alone in this. Every dentist you admire started somewhere. Every financially secure professional was once unsure. You're already doing better than you think.

Your future is still bright. And it's still yours to build—brick by brick, day by day, choice by choice.

Chapter 7: Insurance Essentials for Dentists

Let's be real: insurance isn't the sexiest topic. It doesn't get your heart racing like the idea of buying your dream home or launching your own dental practice. It's not fun like planning a vacation or satisfying like paying off a big debt. But here's the truth: insurance is the quiet backbone of any solid financial plan.

Think of it like this. If your financial life were a building, insurance would be the foundation and the safety net. Without it, all the wealth you're working so hard to build could come crashing down from one unexpected twist of fate. A sudden disability. A malpractice claim. A fire in your office. A health crisis that pulls you away from the chair.

And here's the good news—you don't need to become an expert in insurance to protect yourself. But you do need to understand the basics. You do need to ask smart questions. You do need to make informed decisions.

This chapter will walk you through the essential insurance policies every dentist should consider—what they are, why they matter, how they work, and what to look for. We'll talk about personal coverage, professional liability, business-related protection, and more. By the end of this chapter, you'll feel empowered—not overwhelmed.

Start with This: Why Insurance Matters So Much for Dentists

Let's take a step back. Why does insurance matter so much in dentistry?

Simple. Because your income is high, your hands are your livelihood, and your profession comes with significant legal and financial risk. If something goes wrong—health-wise, legally, professionally—you don't want your career, your family, or your practice to go down with it.

Insurance doesn't just protect your stuff. It protects your future.

1. Disability Insurance: Your Income Lifeline

Let's start with the big one. Disability insurance is arguably the most important policy for any dentist to carry.

Why? Because your ability to work and generate income is your greatest financial asset.

If an accident, injury, or illness keeps you from practicing dentistry—even temporarily—disability insurance steps in to replace a portion of your income.

Types of Disability Coverage:

- **Short-Term Disability**: Covers a few weeks to a few months after an injury or illness
- **Long-Term Disability**: Covers extended periods—sometimes until retirement age

Key Features to Look For:

- **Own-Occupation Definition**: This means you're covered if you can't do *your specific job* as a dentist, even if you can do another job
- **Benefit Period**: How long you'll receive benefits—ideally to age 65 or longer
- **Elimination Period**: The waiting period before benefits begin—often 90 days
- **Monthly Benefit**: Typically covers 60–70% of your gross income

Pros:

- Income protection gives you peace of mind
- Critical for protecting your family's lifestyle

Cons:

- Premiums can be expensive, especially for own-occupation policies
- Complex terms can make policies hard to compare

Action Step: If you don't have disability insurance, get quotes now. If you do have it, review the policy language. Is it truly own-occupation? Are your benefit amounts up to date with your current income?

1. Malpractice Insurance: Your Professional Shield

Also called professional liability insurance, malpractice insurance protects you if a patient sues you for errors, omissions, or negligence in the care you provide.

Even if you did everything right, you can still be sued. And legal defense isn't cheap.

There are two main types:

- **Claims-Made**: Covers claims only if the policy is active both when the incident happened *and* when the claim is made
- **Occurrence-Based**: Covers incidents that happen while the policy is active, regardless of when the claim is filed

Occurrence-based policies tend to be more expensive, but they're more comprehensive and often simpler to manage if you switch jobs or retire.

Pros:

- Essential legal and financial protection
- May be required by law or employer

Cons:

- Doesn't prevent lawsuits—just helps cover them
- Claims-made policies require tail coverage when you cancel

Action Step: Check your current coverage. Are you paying for tail coverage if you leave your employer? If you're buying a practice, understand how malpractice tail coverage transfers or doesn't.

1. Life Insurance: Protection for Those Who Rely on You

If someone depends on your income—a spouse, kids, or even your business partner—you need life insurance.

The goal of life insurance is simple: to provide financial support to your loved ones if you die unexpectedly.

Types:

- **Term Life Insurance**: Covers you for a set period (10, 20, 30 years). Cheaper, straightforward.
- **Whole Life / Permanent Insurance**: Covers you for life and builds cash value. More expensive and complex.

For most dentists, term insurance is the right fit—especially when starting out or raising a family.

How Much Do You Need?

- A common rule is 10x–15x your annual income
- Consider debts, mortgage, education costs, and income replacement needs

Pros:

- Provides peace of mind and protection

- Term life is very affordable for young, healthy individuals

Cons:

- Whole life policies are complex and sometimes oversold
- If you outlive your term policy, there's no payout

Action Step: Calculate how much your family would need to maintain their lifestyle without your income. Get a term life quote. Lock in a rate while you're young and healthy.

1. Business Overhead Insurance: Keep the Lights On

This is one most dentists don't think about until they need it.

If you own a practice and become disabled, business overhead insurance helps cover your ongoing expenses—rent, salaries, utilities, and other fixed costs.

Without this coverage, your practice could go under while you're out recovering.

Pros:

- Buys you time to recover without losing your practice
- Protects your team and patient base

Cons:

- Adds to your monthly costs
- May require medical underwriting

Action Step: If you own a practice or plan to, ask your disability insurance provider about business overhead coverage options.

1. Liability and Umbrella Insurance: Lawsuit Protection Beyond the

Chair

Beyond malpractice, you need personal liability coverage in case someone gets hurt at your home, sues you in a car accident, or files a civil claim unrelated to your dental work.

Umbrella insurance adds extra liability protection on top of your home, auto, and other policies.

Example: If your auto policy covers up to $250,000 and you're sued for $1 million, your umbrella policy covers the gap.

Pros:

- High coverage at relatively low cost
- Covers a wide range of personal liability scenarios

Cons:

- Doesn't replace basic insurance—just extends it

Action Step: Talk to your insurance broker about adding a $1–$3 million umbrella policy. It's inexpensive peace of mind.

1. Health Insurance: The Foundation of Your Safety Net

Whether you're employed, self-employed, or own a practice, health insurance is non-negotiable.

Review your options:

- Employer-provided group plans
- Marketplace plans (especially if self-employed)
- Health Savings Accounts (HSAs) with high-deductible plans

Look for:

- Low out-of-pocket maximums
- Access to quality care providers
- Reasonable premiums

Pros:

- Shields you from catastrophic medical costs
- Can include dental and vision

Cons:

- Can be expensive for high-income self-employed dentists

Action Step: If you're self-employed, talk to a broker to compare plans. Don't just renew your old plan—re-evaluate annually.

1. Property and Equipment Insurance for Practice Owners

If you own a dental practice, your physical space and the equipment inside are some of your biggest investments.

This insurance protects against damage, theft, fire, or natural disasters.

You may also need:

- Business interruption insurance
- Cyber liability insurance (especially if you store patient records digitally)

Action Step: Do a full review of your business insurance policies. Make sure your coverage limits reflect the current replacement cost of your equipment and build-out.

What to Look for in an Insurance Broker or Advisor

Not all insurance agents are created equal. You want someone who:

- Specializes in working with dental professionals
- Can explain policies in plain English
- Isn't pushing products you don't need
- Helps review coverage annually

Action Step: Interview 2–3 insurance professionals before committing. Ask what dentists they've worked with, and how they get paid.

Don't Over-Insure—But Don't Under-Insure Either

It's a balance. You don't need every policy under the sun. But you do need the right coverage in the right amounts for your life stage.

Start with the most essential protections: disability, life, malpractice, health. Then build out with umbrella, property, and business coverage as needed.

Review your policies annually. As your income, family situation, or business evolves, so should your coverage.

Closing Thoughts: Insurance Isn't Just Protection—It's Peace

Insurance isn't exciting. But you know what is? Peace of mind.

Knowing that if something goes wrong, your family's okay. Your practice is okay. Your financial life doesn't unravel.

And here's the beautiful thing about getting your insurance game right: once you've got the right coverage in place, you don't have to think about it every day. You free up energy and headspace to focus on what really matters—your patients, your business, your family, your future.

So breathe. You don't have to get it all figured out today. But you do need to start.

Make the call. Book the appointment. Read the fine print. Ask the questions.

Then move forward with confidence—knowing you're building a life of stability, intention, and resilience.

Chapter 8: Investing and Wealth-Building Basics

Let's start with a deep breath.

Because if the word "investing" brings up stress, fear, or even a twinge of guilt—you're not alone. Most dentists didn't grow up talking about stocks at the dinner table. You didn't get investment training in dental school. And yet, here you are, responsible for not just earning a high income—but turning that income into real wealth.

That's the whole point of this chapter: to help you bridge that gap between working for your money and having your money work for you. Investing is how you build lasting freedom. It's how you retire with dignity. It's how you protect your family and fund your dreams.

And you don't have to be perfect. You just have to begin.

Why Dentists Have Unique Wealth-Building Challenges

Let's name the elephant in the room: dentists start their careers at a disadvantage in some key financial ways:

- You finish school later than many other professionals
- You often graduate with significant debt
- Your income starts high but so do your expenses
- You may feel pressure to "look the part" with a nice house, car, or practice early on

These factors delay your ability to invest, and that delay costs you something powerful: **compound interest.**

But here's the upside. You also have a big earning potential, strong job security, and the ability to course-correct quickly with the right plan.

This chapter is that plan.

The Big Picture: What Is Wealth?

Wealth isn't just about the size of your bank account. It's about freedom. Options. Peace of mind. The ability to make choices not out of desperation—but from a place of strength.

Wealth is having your money support your life, not the other way around.

And wealth-building means:

- Living below your means
- Consistently saving and investing
- Protecting your assets
- Thinking long-term

It's boring. It's methodical. And it works.

How Investing Works: A Dentist's Plain-English Guide

Investing is the act of putting your money into something (stocks, bonds, real estate, etc.) with the expectation that it will grow in value over time.

The most common place dentists invest is in the **stock market.** When you invest in the market, you're buying ownership in companies. If those companies grow and earn profits, your investments (shares) usually increase in value. You may also earn dividends—payouts from company profits.

The power of investing comes from something called **compound growth.**

Here's an example:

- If you invest $500/month starting at age 30, and it earns 7% a year, by age 60 you'll have over $600,000
- If you wait until age 40 to start, you'll have less than half that—around $280,000

Time is the key ingredient. And the earlier you start, the better.

Where to Begin: The Three Buckets of Investing

You can organize your investing into three main buckets:

1. **Tax-Advantaged Retirement Accounts**
2. **Taxable Brokerage Accounts**
3. **Practice or Business Investment**

Let's break each one down.

1. Tax-Advantaged Retirement Accounts

These accounts are designed by the government to encourage you to save for retirement. The two most common types are:

- **401(k)/403(b)/SIMPLE IRA**: Often offered through employers or group practices
- **Traditional IRA or Roth IRA**: Individual retirement accounts

Traditional = tax-deferred. You deduct contributions today, but pay taxes when you withdraw in retirement.

Roth = after-tax. You pay taxes now, but growth and withdrawals are tax-free in retirement.

For many dentists, a Roth IRA early in your career and a 401(k) or profit-sharing plan later make a great combination.

Contribution Limits (2025)

- Roth/Traditional IRA: $7,000 ($8,000 if over 50)
- 401(k): $23,000 ($30,000 if over 50)

Pros:

- Tax benefits boost long-term growth

- Some accounts come with employer matches

Cons:

- Penalties for early withdrawal
- Annual contribution limits

Action Step: Open a Roth IRA if you haven't already. If you're in practice, talk to your CPA or advisor about setting up a 401(k) or profit-sharing plan.

1. Taxable Brokerage Accounts

Once you max out your tax-advantaged accounts, the next place to invest is a **taxable brokerage account.**

You can invest in anything here—stocks, mutual funds, ETFs, even real estate investment trusts (REITs).

This account doesn't have tax benefits, but it also doesn't have contribution limits. It's flexible, accessible, and great for:

- Mid-term goals (buying a building, early retirement)
- Supplementing retirement income

Pros:

- No contribution limits
- Funds can be accessed anytime

Cons:

- You pay taxes on dividends and capital gains
- Requires more tracking and planning

Action Step: Open a brokerage account with a reputable firm (Fidelity, Schwab, Vanguard). Start with a monthly auto-transfer—even $250/month adds up.

1. Practice or Business Investment

If you own your practice, you have a unique third bucket of wealth: **business equity.**

This is different from stocks or funds. It's riskier—but also potentially more rewarding.

Growing your practice can include:

- Upgrading technology
- Expanding locations
- Hiring associates
- Increasing marketing

Each of these investments should be evaluated like any other: will this grow revenue? Will it increase profit? What's the ROI?

Action Step: Track your practice's profit margins, revenue per chair, and net income annually. Treat your practice like an investment.

What Should You Invest In?

Start simple. Diversify. Avoid hype.

A good beginner portfolio includes:

- **Index Funds**: These track the overall market (like the S&P 500)
- **Target-Date Funds**: Automatically adjust your risk as you approach retirement
- **ETFs**: Low-cost, diversified investments

You don't need to pick individual stocks. In fact, most people who try to beat the market end up losing to it.

Action Step: Choose a target-date retirement fund for simplicity, or build a portfolio of 3–4 diversified index funds. Automate your contributions.

What About Real Estate?

Many dentists consider real estate a part of their long-term plan. This could include:

- Buying the building where your practice operates
- Owning rental properties
- Investing in REITs (real estate investment trusts)

Real estate can be a great diversifier, but it comes with:

- Property management headaches
- Market risks
- Capital requirements

Pros:

- Tangible asset
- Tax advantages (depreciation, 1031 exchanges)

Cons:

- Illiquid
- High upfront cost
- Active management needed (unless using property managers)

Action Step: If you're considering real estate, run the numbers carefully. Work with a CPA to evaluate tax implications. Start small.

Investing vs. Speculation

There's a difference between investing and gambling. Investing is long-term, patient, and strategic. Speculation is betting on quick gains.

Examples of speculation:

- Day trading
- Cryptocurrency hype
- Hot stock tips

As a dentist, you don't have time to watch the markets daily. And you don't need to. Set up a simple, diversified portfolio and stick with it.

Action Step: Unfollow financial influencers who push hype. Stick to boring, proven strategies.

How Much Should You Invest?

Here's a rough guideline:

- Start by saving at least **15–20% of your gross income** toward retirement
- If you're late to the game, consider bumping that to **25–30%**
- Include debt payments and cash reserves in your plan too

Action Step: Calculate your current savings rate. If you're under 15%, increase by 1–2% every quarter until you hit your target.

Who Should Help You?

You don't have to do this alone. A great financial advisor can:

- Help you build a custom investment plan
- Keep you disciplined through market ups and downs
- Coordinate with your CPA and estate attorney

Look for:

- Fee-only fiduciaries (they work in your best interest)
- Experience with dental professionals
- Transparent pricing

Action Step: Interview two financial advisors this year. Ask how they'd build a plan for someone in your exact situation.

The Emotional Side of Investing

Money is emotional. And investing can stir up anxiety—especially during market dips.

Here's what you need to remember:

- **Markets go up and down.** Stay invested anyway.
- **You can't time the market.** But time *in* the market works.
- **Don't panic sell.** That's how people lock in losses.

Build your plan when things are calm. Stick to it when things get turbulent.

Action Step: Write an "investment mission statement." Something like: "I invest consistently to build freedom and peace for my family. I focus on long-term growth, not short-term noise."

Closing Thoughts: Wealth Isn't Built in a Day

Let this be your reminder:

You don't have to know everything. You just have to get started.

You don't need a perfect plan. You just need a consistent one.

And you don't have to build wealth the way anyone else does. You get to define what wealth means for you.

So start where you are. Set up the Roth IRA. Contribute to your 401(k). Talk to a trusted advisor. Open the brokerage account. Review your practice as an asset.

Do one thing this week to invest in your future.

Because smart investing isn't about chasing trends. It's about building a life that supports your values, your freedom, and your future.

Chapter 9: Managing Credit, Debt, and Your Financial Profile

Let's talk about something that makes almost everyone a little uncomfortable—debt.

If you're a dentist, you've probably carried or are currently carrying more debt than most people will see in a lifetime. Student loans. Business loans. Equipment leases. A mortgage. Maybe a car note. Credit cards. It adds up fast.

And yet here's the truth: debt is not your enemy. But unmanaged debt? That's a different story.

This chapter is about turning debt into something you control, not something that controls you. It's about learning how credit works—because your credit score isn't just a number. It's a tool. And like any tool, when used wisely, it can help you build something great.

You don't have to be perfect. You don't have to eliminate all debt to be financially successful. But you do need to understand how it fits into the bigger picture—and how to manage it strategically.

Understanding the Role of Debt in Dentistry

Let's start with the big picture. Dentists carry a unique kind of financial burden:

- High cost of education (often $200,000+)
- Costly practice ownership options
- Expensive equipment and technology

- Professional liability considerations

Debt is part of the journey. But it shouldn't define your future.

The goal isn't necessarily to be debt-free. The goal is to be financially free—to have control, options, peace.

That means:

- Using credit wisely
- Managing loan payments strategically
- Knowing your numbers
- Protecting your credit profile

Let's break it down.

What Is Credit, Really?

Credit is your ability to borrow money based on trust that you'll pay it back. Your **credit score** is essentially your financial reputation. Lenders use it to decide if they'll loan you money, how much, and at what interest rate.

Your credit profile is made up of:

- Your credit score (typically 300 to 850)
- Your credit report (a detailed history of your credit activity)

Credit Scores Are Calculated Based On:

1. **Payment History (35%)** – Do you pay on time?
2. **Amounts Owed (30%)** – How much of your available credit are you using?
3. **Length of Credit History (15%)** – How long have you had credit?
4. **Credit Mix (10%)** – Do you have different types of credit (cards, loans, mortgage)?
5. **New Credit (10%)** – Are you opening too many new accounts?

Why Your Credit Score Matters as a Dentist

As a dentist, your credit score can impact:

- Your ability to buy a home
- Your interest rate on a practice loan
- Your lease terms for equipment or real estate
- Your ability to refinance student loans

Even insurance companies and some employers check credit.

Higher credit score = lower interest rates = more money in your pocket.

A small score difference (like 720 vs. 780) can mean tens of thousands saved over the life of a loan.

Action Steps to Improve Your Credit Score

1. **Check your credit report** (free at AnnualCreditReport.com)
2. **Pay your bills on time**—set up autopay to avoid missed payments
3. **Keep credit utilization under 30%**—if your card limit is $10,000, try not to carry a balance over $3,000
4. **Don't close old accounts**—long history helps
5. **Avoid opening too many accounts quickly**—space out credit pulls

Student Loan Strategy

If you're carrying dental school debt, you're not alone. The average dental student graduates with $250,000+ in loans.

Here's the good news: that debt doesn't have to derail your financial goals. But it does need a plan.

There are three main paths:

1. **Aggressive Payoff** – Pay off debt as quickly as possible
2. **Strategic Refinance** – Refinance to lower interest, keep flexible terms
3. **Income-Driven Repayment / Forgiveness** – Useful if you work in public service or plan to stay in a lower-income job

Pros of Aggressive Payoff:

- Less interest paid over time
- Faster financial freedom

Cons:

- Delays investing and saving
- Less cash flow flexibility

Action Step: Know your exact balance, interest rates, and loan types. Use tools like the federal loan simulator to map your options. Pick a strategy and review it yearly.

Business Debt: Good Debt vs. Bad Debt

Not all debt is created equal.

Good debt:

- Grows your income or assets
- Has manageable payments and fair terms
- Includes business loans for practice expansion, real estate, or equipment

Bad debt:

- Drains your cash flow with no return
- Has high interest rates
- Includes credit cards, payday loans, unnecessary consumer debt

Debt used to grow your practice or invest in yourself strategically isn't inherently bad. But every loan should be evaluated with a clear ROI.

Action Step: Before taking on any new business debt, ask: Will this increase revenue? Can I afford the payments? What's the break-even point?

Credit Cards: Useful or Dangerous?

Credit cards are neither good nor bad—they're a tool. The danger comes when they're used for emotional spending or become a habit without a payoff plan.

Smart Ways Dentists Use Credit Cards:

- To earn rewards on business expenses
- To track spending for bookkeeping
- For short-term financing with 0% APR cards

Risks to Watch:

- Carrying balances month to month
- Letting multiple cards spiral out of control
- Using credit as a substitute for cash flow

Action Step: Keep credit cards below 30% utilization. Pay in full each month. Set alerts for due dates.

Building and Protecting Your Financial Profile

Your financial profile is more than just credit. It's the total picture of how you manage money. It includes:

- Your income and expenses
- Your debt and credit
- Your net worth
- Your financial habits

Think of your financial profile like your clinical reputation. It's built slowly, tested under pressure, and reflects your ability to handle responsibility.

To protect it:

- Use strong passwords and two-factor authentication
- Monitor your credit reports for fraud

- Shred documents with personal info
- Don't co-sign loans for others

Action Step: Sign up for a credit monitoring service. Place fraud alerts if you've ever been exposed to a breach.

What Lenders Look For

If you're applying for a loan—home, business, equipment—lenders evaluate a few key things:

1. **Credit Score** – Are you responsible with borrowed money?
2. **Debt-to-Income Ratio (DTI)** – Can you afford more debt?
3. **Cash Flow** – Is your income steady?
4. **Assets and Collateral** – What do you own?
5. **Business Plan (if applicable)** – Is your practice financially sound?

Action Step: Run your own numbers before a lender does. Know your DTI. Prepare your documents (tax returns, P&L, bank statements).

Dealing with Debt Stress

Money stress is real—and heavy. Especially for dentists who feel like they're supposed to "have it together."

You might feel:

- Guilty for having so much debt
- Overwhelmed by monthly payments
- Embarrassed to talk to a professional

But here's the truth: talking to a financial planner, debt counselor, or advisor isn't a sign of failure—it's a step toward freedom.

Action Step: If you're losing sleep over debt, talk to someone. Not a sales pitch—someone who truly wants to help.

The Power of a Financial Reset

Sometimes you need a reset. Maybe your spending has crept up. Maybe you've ignored credit scores or minimum payments too long.

A reset can include:

- Creating a real budget
- Making a debt snowball or avalanche plan
- Consolidating debt strategically
- Selling unused stuff to free up cash

It's never too late to change course.

Action Step: Block off 2 hours this week. Review your finances with no distractions. Make one decision that moves you toward stability.

Closing Thoughts: You're Not Defined by Debt

Debt does not make you irresponsible.

A low credit score does not make you a failure.

What matters is that you take ownership of your financial story, starting now. One step at a time. One choice at a time.

Because every dentist who's financially free today once sat where you are. With questions. With debt. With doubt.

But they kept going. And you can too.

Your future is still wide open.

With clarity, intention, and courage—you'll get there.

Chapter 10: Advanced Financial Planning as You Gain Experience

Let's take a moment to acknowledge something important: You've come a long way.

If you're reading this chapter, you've likely moved past the early turbulence of dental school debt, initial practice challenges, and figuring out how to get your personal finances in order. That doesn't mean things are easy—but it does mean you're no longer in survival mode. You're building something.

Maybe you're earning a consistent income. Maybe you own your practice—or several. Maybe you're investing, saving, managing a team, or supporting a family. You've reached a place where your decisions aren't just about getting by. They're about what comes next.

This chapter is about what comes next.

It's about stepping into your role as the architect of your financial life—refining, optimizing, and expanding what you've built so far. It's not about perfection. It's about planning with purpose.

Let's dig in.

What Is Advanced Financial Planning?

Advanced financial planning means going beyond the basics of budgeting, saving, and debt management. It's about:

- Structuring your income for tax efficiency
- Making intentional decisions about practice growth and ownership

- Strategizing long-term investments
- Creating multi-layered protection plans
- Planning for kids' education, your legacy, and eventually, retirement

It's about aligning your money with your life—so your financial plan supports what matters most to you.

And most importantly? It's about staying proactive instead of reactive.

Step One: Create a Financial Roadmap

Let's start by zooming out. Where are you trying to go?

A financial roadmap includes:

- Your short-term goals (1–3 years)
- Your mid-term goals (3–10 years)
- Your long-term vision (10+ years)

Examples:

- Paying off all business debt in 5 years
- Buying a second location in 3 years
- Funding your kids' college education
- Retiring by age 60
- Traveling three months a year post-practice

Action Step: Take 30 minutes this week to write out your top 3 financial goals in each category. This becomes the compass for your planning.

Optimizing Your Income: Tax Strategy and Income Structuring

As a mid-career or experienced dentist, your income is likely your biggest financial engine. But how you structure and use that income can dramatically affect your long-term wealth.

Considerations:

- Are you still filing as a sole proprietor—or have you transitioned to an S-corp?

- Are you taking advantage of all deductions available to practice owners?
- Are you using retirement plans to lower taxable income?

Common tax-saving strategies for dentists:

- Max out a 401(k) and profit-sharing plan
- Set up a defined benefit plan (for high earners)
- Deduct business travel and CE properly
- Claim depreciation on equipment and real estate

Pros:

- More after-tax income stays in your pocket
- Creates efficiency as income grows

Cons:

- Requires strong coordination with your CPA
- May need to restructure business entity

Action Step: Schedule a mid-year tax planning meeting with your CPA—not just a review in April. Ask about opportunities specific to your profession.

Growing Practice Equity: Expansion, Efficiency, and Exit Strategy

For many dentists, your practice is your largest asset outside your home. So, how are you treating it?

As you gain experience, you may consider:

- Adding associates
- Expanding to a second location
- Buying out partners
- Selling your practice (eventually)

Each of these decisions comes with financial, tax, and lifestyle implications.

Key Metrics to Watch:

- EBITDA (earnings before interest, taxes, depreciation, and amortization)
- Net profit margin
- Collections per provider
- Overhead percentage

Questions to Ask:

- Is my practice scalable?
- Are my systems documented and efficient?
- Am I grooming an associate to take over?

Action Step: Get an annual valuation of your practice. Not just for sale prep—but to track your growth and net worth.

Building Multi-Layered Investment Strategies

Once you're contributing consistently to retirement accounts, it's time to think bigger.

Advanced investment planning includes:

- Diversifying across tax buckets (taxable, tax-deferred, tax-free)
- Investing in alternative assets (real estate, private equity)
- Using trusts or family LLCs to structure long-term wealth
- Dollar-cost averaging vs. lump-sum investing strategies

Pros:

- Reduces reliance on one income stream or account
- Helps plan for different life stages (college, retirement, legacy)

Cons:

- More complexity = more oversight needed

Action Step: Create a spreadsheet with your current asset allocation and account types. Then ask your advisor: how can I diversify further?

Advanced Risk Management: Beyond the Basics

As your wealth grows, so does your need to protect it.

In addition to standard insurance (disability, malpractice, health), consider:

- Umbrella policies over $1M
- Entity structuring to separate personal and business liability
- Life insurance as a wealth transfer tool
- Buy-sell agreements with partners

Don't forget cyber liability and employment practices insurance—especially if you have a team.

Action Step: Meet with an insurance specialist to audit your coverage. Ask: where am I underinsured or exposed?

Estate Planning and Wealth Transfer

Even if you're not thinking about legacy yet, you should be. Estate planning isn't just about dying—it's about making sure your wishes are honored and your loved ones are protected.

Essentials:

- A will
- Power of attorney
- Healthcare directive
- Trust (revocable or irrevocable, depending on complexity)

For practice owners:

- Clear succession plan
- Estate tax strategies

- Life insurance to cover estate liquidity needs

Pros:

- Prevents legal battles and delays
- Protects heirs and practice staff

Cons:

- Upfront legal costs
- Needs updating as your life evolves

Action Step: If you don't have an estate plan, create one this year. If you do—review and update it every 3 years or after any major life change.

Kids, College, and Cash Flow

If you have children, you've probably thought about how to fund their education. But don't let college derail your own financial goals.

Options:

- 529 college savings plans
- UTMA accounts
- Trusts for future expenses
- Teaching your kids to work and save early

Key advice: take care of your retirement first. You can borrow for college—not for retirement.

Action Step: Estimate future college costs and run a plan. Then decide how much you want to contribute monthly—and automate it.

Planning for Partial Retirement or Phased Transitions

Not every dentist wants to go from full-time to full-stop.

More and more experienced dentists are planning:

- Part-time work in their 60s

- Consulting or mentoring roles
- Practice ownership without clinical duties
- Lifestyle design: travel, family, creative pursuits

This requires planning not just for money—but for time.

Questions to ask:

- What does my ideal retirement look like?
- How much income will I need monthly?
- What will I do with my time?

Action Step: Build a financial model of partial retirement. What would it cost to scale back by 20%? 50%? What could you cut, automate, or outsource?

Managing Burnout, Lifestyle Creep, and Emotional Spending

By now, you've realized financial planning isn't just numbers. It's emotional.

Burnout, stress, lifestyle inflation, comparison—it all affects your choices.

You may:

- Feel pressure to maintain a certain image
- Spend to cope with stress
- Delay your own goals to "reward" your hard work

This is normal. But it's also worth examining.

Action Step: Review your last 3 months of spending. Are you funding your values—or your stress relief? Adjust intentionally.

Building a Team of Advisors

You don't have to do this alone.

At this stage, your financial life deserves:

- A financial advisor who understands dentistry
- A proactive CPA

- An estate planning attorney
- A business or practice consultant
- An insurance broker with access to multiple carriers

Action Step: Schedule annual team meetings. Let your advisors coordinate—so your plan is integrated.

Closing Thoughts: You're the CEO of Your Life

This stage of your career comes with more complexity—but also more possibility.

You're not just a dentist. You're a leader. An investor. A business owner. A partner. A parent. A planner.

And when you plan your finances with the same care and clarity you bring to your clinical work—everything changes.

You stop reacting. You start designing. You stop drifting. You start directing. You stop surviving. You start thriving.

Take one step this week. Call your CPA. Schedule that advisor meeting. Review your roadmap.

You're not alone. You're not behind. You're exactly where you're supposed to be—and your future is still wide open.

Chapter 11: Estate Planning for Dental Professionals

Let's start with the uncomfortable part: one day, you won't be here. It's a hard truth, but it's also a powerful motivator. Because the reality of death is not just about loss—it's about opportunity. The opportunity to make things easier for the people you love. To ensure your life's work and your hard-earned wealth go where you want them to go. To protect your patients, your practice, your family, and your legacy.

That's what estate planning is really about.

It's not just a bunch of legal documents or something to deal with when you're older. It's a financial system designed to protect what you've built—and the people you built it for.

So whether you're just starting out or already years into your practice, this chapter is for you. We're going to walk through everything you need to know—clearly, calmly, and compassionately. No guilt. No jargon. Just wisdom, action steps, and a way forward.

What Is Estate Planning?

Estate planning is the process of organizing your financial and legal affairs so that your assets—everything from your home to your practice to your investments—are handled according to your wishes after you pass away or become incapacitated.

It's not just for the ultra-wealthy. If you have a bank account, a business, a home, or a family—you need an estate plan.

At its core, estate planning answers three big questions:

1. Who will inherit your assets?
2. Who will manage your affairs if you can't?
3. How can you reduce stress, taxes, and delays for your loved ones?

Estate planning isn't about fear. It's about love. It's a final act of care for your family, your patients, your business, and your legacy.

Why Estate Planning Matters So Much for Dentists

As a dental professional, you face some unique estate planning needs:

- You likely have significant assets tied up in your practice
- You may have young children or a spouse who relies on your income
- You may have student loans or business loans to resolve
- You likely have a high income and a growing net worth

Without a plan in place, your family could be left with:

- Delays in probate court
- Tax burdens they weren't prepared for
- Confusion about how to run, sell, or wind down your practice
- Family conflict over inheritances

Let's make sure that doesn't happen.

The Core Components of an Estate Plan

There are five essential elements to every strong estate plan:

1. A will
2. A power of attorney
3. A healthcare directive
4. A trust (in many cases)
5. A practice succession plan (for practice owners)

Let's break these down.

1. The Will: Your Voice When You're Gone

A **will** is a legal document that states who should inherit your assets after you die and who should carry out your wishes (your executor).

In your will, you can:

- Name guardians for minor children
- Distribute specific assets
- Make charitable donations
- Outline funeral wishes (optional)

Without a will, the state decides who gets what—and it rarely matches what you'd want.

Action Step: Hire an estate planning attorney to draft a will that reflects your current life, family, and values. Update it every 3–5 years or after any major life change.

1. Power of Attorney: Who Speaks for You If You Can't?

A **power of attorney (POA)** is someone you appoint to manage your financial affairs if you become incapacitated.

They can:

- Pay bills
- Manage bank accounts
- Sign documents
- Make financial decisions on your behalf

There are two types:

- **Durable POA** (for financial matters)
- **Medical POA** (for healthcare decisions)

Action Step: Choose someone you deeply trust. Someone organized, calm, and capable. Not necessarily a family member—just the right person.

1. Healthcare Directive: Your Medical Wishes, Clearly Stated

Also called a **living will** or **advance directive**, this document outlines what kind of medical care you want—or don't want—if you're unable to speak for yourself.

You can include:

- Do-not-resuscitate (DNR) instructions
- End-of-life care preferences
- Organ donation choices

Action Step: Talk through these wishes with your spouse, partner, or close family. Then have them documented with your attorney.

1. Trusts: Control, Protection, and Privacy

A **trust** is a legal structure that holds and manages your assets according to specific rules you set.

There are many kinds of trusts, but the most common for dentists are:

- **Revocable Living Trusts**: Let you retain control while alive; avoids probate
- **Irrevocable Trusts**: Offers stronger asset protection; cannot be changed easily
- **Minor Trusts**: Protect assets for children until a certain age

Benefits of trusts:

- Avoid probate (saving time and legal fees)
- Keep your affairs private (unlike wills, which are public record)

- Protect heirs from creditors, divorce, or poor money decisions

Action Step: If your estate is over $1 million (including practice value), talk to an attorney about setting up a living trust. It's not just for the ultra-wealthy.

1. Practice Succession Planning

This is the part many dentists skip. Don't.

If you own a practice, your death or disability leaves patients, staff, and your business in limbo—unless you have a plan.

Your succession plan should include:

- A named successor or emergency management plan
- Instructions for temporary practice closure or sale
- Clear ownership transition terms (especially if you have partners)
- Access to passwords, records, insurance, payroll

Real-World Example: A mid-career dentist passed unexpectedly without a succession plan. His spouse had to scramble to maintain the practice's value, while dealing with grief and legal issues. With a plan, the practice could've been sold quickly and fairly—with less stress and more financial return.

Action Step: Work with your CPA, attorney, and a practice broker to develop a written succession plan. Review it annually.

Advanced Estate Planning Tools

For higher net-worth dentists or those with complex family dynamics, consider:

- **Charitable trusts** – support causes you care about, while reducing estate taxes
- **Family limited partnerships (FLPs)** – structure wealth transfer efficiently

- **Irrevocable Life Insurance Trusts (ILITs)** – keep insurance outside of taxable estate
- **Generation-skipping trusts** – provide for grandchildren and preserve legacy

Action Step: Ask your estate planning attorney: Which advanced tools make sense for my situation?

Handling Debts and Taxes After Death

Many dentists wonder: What happens to my student loans or practice debt when I die?

Here's the breakdown:

- **Federal student loans** are discharged at death
- **Private loans** may not be—depends on lender terms
- **Practice debt** may become part of your estate obligations

To cover these, life insurance is key.

Action Step: Review your debts. Do you have enough life insurance to cover them and still leave something behind?

Don't Forget Digital Assets

More and more, your digital life needs estate planning too:

- Email and social media accounts
- Practice management software logins
- Cloud storage and digital photos
- Cryptocurrency keys

Action Step: Create a digital asset inventory. Include access instructions, passwords (stored securely), and name a digital executor in your estate plan.

Talking About It: Estate Planning Conversations That Matter

One of the hardest parts of estate planning isn't creating the documents—it's talking about them.

Conversations to consider:

- With your spouse or partner
- With your kids (if age appropriate)
- With your practice partners
- With your chosen POA or executor

Tips:

- Schedule a time, don't spring it on them
- Focus on love and protection, not doom and gloom
- Provide clear documents and instructions

Action Step: Pick one person to talk to this week about your estate plan. Break the ice. Get it started.

Keeping It Updated

Life changes. Your estate plan should too.

Update your documents if:

- You get married, divorced, or have a child
- You move to a different state
- Your net worth significantly increases
- A beneficiary dies or becomes incapacitated

Action Step: Set a calendar reminder to review your estate plan every 3 years—or sooner if major life events occur.

Closing Thoughts: Estate Planning Is an Act of Love

Estate planning isn't about fear. It's about peace.

It's not about controlling people from the grave. It's about making their lives easier when things are hardest.

As a dentist, you've worked too hard—and helped too many people—to leave your legacy to chance.

So take the step. Make the call. Review the documents.

Because your family, your patients, your staff, and your future self will thank you.

This isn't just about money. It's about meaning. It's about making sure everything you built continues to serve those you love.

Part 2: Building a Career – From Associate to Ownership

Part 2 of *Financial Literacy For Dentists* shifts from the classroom to the clinic—where real-world experience, career decisions, and financial growth begin to take shape. This section guides dentists through the crucial transition from new associate to seasoned practice owner, breaking down both the opportunities and pitfalls that can define the next phase of a dental career.

We begin by exploring the associate years—how to evaluate job offers, understand compensation models (salary, percentage of production, collections-based pay), and make the most of employer-provided benefits. We offer clear, practical advice for contract negotiation, knowing your worth, and avoiding common first-job traps that can limit growth. These years are not just about surviving—they're about positioning yourself for long-term success.

As career experience builds, so do questions about the future: Should you stay an associate or pursue ownership? Do you buy into an existing practice, start your own, or become a partner? Part 2 walks you through each of these paths with a focus on financial implications, risk management, and lifestyle alignment. We explore loan structures for buying a practice, how to assess a practice's value, and what it really takes to manage not just clinical care, but employees, vendors, marketing, and overhead.

This section also addresses:

- Setting financial goals that evolve with your career
- Saving and investing while growing your income
- Building business acumen to complement clinical expertise
- Understanding the personal vs. professional financial split as an owner

Whether you're a few years into your career or ready to take the leap into ownership, Part 2 equips you with a roadmap. It's about more than choosing a title—it's about building a career that works for your life, your finances, and your vision for the future.

By the end of this section, readers will feel empowered to take strategic, confident steps toward building a thriving career—and to do it without sacrificing their financial peace of mind along the way.

40

Chapter 12: Financial Planning With a Spouse or Partner

Money is emotional.

It touches every part of our lives—our sense of safety, freedom, identity, and legacy. And when you share your life with someone—whether it's a spouse, a committed partner, or a long-term relationship—money isn't just personal anymore. It's shared. It's tangled. It's part of how you love each other, support each other, and plan your future together.

And let's be honest: that can get messy.

This chapter is about navigating that mess—with grace, clarity, and a sense of teamwork. Because while money can cause tension in relationships, it can also become a source of trust, connection, and shared vision.

So whether you're in a new relationship, raising kids together, managing a practice as a couple, or recovering from past financial stress—this chapter is here to help you plan, grow, and thrive together.

Why Financial Planning As a Couple Matters So Much

You may already know this, but it's worth stating clearly:

Money fights are one of the leading causes of relationship stress—and even divorce.

But here's the flip side: couples who talk openly about money, plan together, and build shared goals tend to have stronger, more resilient partnerships.

Because at the end of the day, it's not just about the dollars. It's about:

- How you make decisions
- How you handle stress
- How you honor each other's dreams
- How you build your life together

And that takes more than spreadsheets. It takes conversations. Clarity. Compassion.

Start With the Conversation, Not the Numbers

Before you build a financial plan as a couple, you need to build a foundation of trust and communication.

That starts with a simple question: What does money mean to each of you?

Talk through:

- How money was handled in your families growing up
- Your earliest memories of money
- Your financial fears and goals
- What financial success looks like to you

You'll learn a lot—not just about money, but about each other.

Action Step: Set aside one hour for a "money story" conversation. Each partner shares their background, beliefs, and feelings about money—with no judgment, just curiosity.

Build a Shared Financial Vision

Once you've opened the door to real conversation, it's time to talk vision. Ask:

- What kind of lifestyle do we want?
- How do we define financial security?
- What are our short-term, mid-term, and long-term goals?
- How do we want to handle big decisions—like home buying, kids' education, or retirement?

Then put it in writing. Not a contract—but a compass.

Action Step: Create a joint financial vision statement. Something like: "We want to live comfortably, raise our kids with stability, pay off our debt in five years, and retire by 60 with the ability to travel."

Decide How to Combine (or Separate) Finances

There's no one-size-fits-all approach to managing money as a couple. You have options:

1. **Fully Combined:** All income and expenses go into shared accounts
2. **Partially Combined:** Shared accounts for joint expenses, separate accounts for personal spending
3. **Completely Separate:** Each partner manages their own money and contributes to shared costs

Each has pros and cons.

Fully Combined Pros:

- Total transparency
- Easier to manage shared goals

Cons:

- Can feel like a loss of autonomy
- One partner may feel more control or more burden

Partially Combined Pros:

- Balance of togetherness and independence
- Easier to budget for joint expenses

Cons:

- Requires communication and coordination

- Can lead to misunderstandings about fairness

Action Step: Choose the system that feels most aligned with your values and personalities. Revisit the decision annually or after major life changes.

Create a Household Budget—Together

No matter how you split your accounts, you need a plan for how money flows in your household.

That means:

- Knowing your total monthly income (after taxes)
- Listing fixed expenses (mortgage, insurance, loan payments)
- Estimating variable expenses (groceries, gas, entertainment)
- Setting aside money for goals (saving, investing, vacation)

Action Step: Schedule a monthly "money date" to review income, expenses, and progress toward shared goals. Keep it short and friendly—coffee or wine optional.

Addressing Debt As a Couple

Debt can bring shame, secrecy, and strain. But it can also be a chance to show up for each other.

Start with transparency:

- List all debts: student loans, credit cards, car notes, business loans
- Discuss repayment strategies
- Decide whether debt will be paid together or separately

If one partner is a dentist: It's common for the dentist to carry significant student or business debt. Be open about how that will impact joint financial plans.

Action Step: Create a joint debt strategy. Will you tackle high-interest debt first? Refinance? Pay aggressively or strategically?

Planning for Unequal Incomes

In many dental households, one partner earns significantly more than the other. This can lead to:

- Power dynamics
- Guilt or resentment
- Pressure to contribute equally, even if it's not realistic

Solutions:

- Share decisions, not just dollars
- Divide expenses by percentage of income, not 50/50
- Respect non-financial contributions (childcare, home management)

Action Step: Have an honest conversation about how each partner contributes—and what "fair" looks like in your relationship.

Aligning on Saving and Investing

Now the fun part: growing your wealth.

Decide:

- How much you want to save each month
- What retirement accounts you'll use (401(k), IRA, Roth)
- Whether you'll invest jointly or separately
- How much risk you're both comfortable with

Don't forget emergency savings, college savings, and long-term care planning.

Action Step: Work with a financial advisor to build a plan that reflects both of your goals. Make sure each partner understands the investment strategy.

Insurance and Protection Planning

Protecting each other means planning for the unexpected.

Make sure you both have:

- Health insurance

- Disability insurance (especially for the dentist)
- Life insurance (term is often best)
- Umbrella liability insurance

If you own a practice: Your partner should know how to access policies, contacts, and key business information in case something happens to you.

Action Step: Create a "family financial binder" or secure digital folder with all insurance policies, passwords, and emergency contacts.

Estate Planning as a Couple

Estate planning isn't just about dying—it's about making sure your wishes are honored and your partner is protected.

Every couple should have:

- A will
- Powers of attorney (financial and medical)
- Healthcare directives
- Beneficiary designations on all accounts

Action Step: Meet with an estate planning attorney. Update your documents every 3–5 years—or after any major life change.

Planning for Children and Family Support

If you have kids—or plan to—you'll need to plan for:

- Daycare or schooling costs
- College savings (529 plans)
- Custody and guardianship arrangements

Also consider:

- Supporting aging parents
- Blended family dynamics
- Helping family without sacrificing your goals

Action Step: Have regular check-ins about family priorities. What are you willing to pay for? What boundaries do you want to set?

Working Together in the Practice

If your spouse or partner works with you in the dental practice, it adds another layer of complexity.

Discuss:

- Roles and responsibilities
- Compensation and benefits
- Decision-making authority
- What happens if the relationship changes or ends

Consider a formal partnership agreement—even if you're married.

Action Step: Meet with your CPA and attorney to document roles and expectations. Protect both your business and your relationship.

Handling Financial Conflict

Disagreements will happen. That's normal.

The goal isn't to eliminate conflict—it's to handle it constructively.

Tips:

- Don't avoid money conversations
- Use "I" statements, not blame
- Focus on solving problems together
- Set regular financial check-ins to prevent tension

Action Step: Choose a recurring time to talk about money—not when you're tired, stressed, or already arguing. Keep it consistent.

Getting Professional Help

If money issues are causing stress, confusion, or conflict—get help.

A great financial advisor can:

- Help you build a joint plan
- Mediate differences in goals or risk tolerance

- Coordinate with your CPA and estate attorney

A therapist or coach can:

- Help you unpack money dynamics
- Improve communication and trust
- Address deeper emotional patterns around money

Action Step: If money feels like a source of friction in your relationship, don't wait. Reach out for support early.

Closing Thoughts: Money as a Team Sport

At the end of the day, financial planning with a spouse or partner is about one thing: building a life together.

It's not about one person taking control. It's about walking side by side.

Yes, there will be challenges. There will be trade-offs. But there will also be connection, celebration, and shared wins.

And when your money serves your relationship—not the other way around—everything changes.

So talk. Plan. Listen. Adjust. Dream big.

You're not alone. And your future is still wide open.

Chapter 13: Planning for Life Beyond Dentistry

Let's start with a truth that's easy to ignore when you're deep in the day-to-day grind: Your career in dentistry is just one chapter of your life.

It might be a big chapter. It might be the chapter that's brought you purpose, income, and identity. But it's not the whole book.

One day, whether by choice or by force—your time practicing dentistry will come to an end.

And the question is: What comes next?

That's what this chapter is all about. Not just retiring from dentistry—but retiring into something meaningful. Whether it's a second act, a new identity, or simply a softer pace of life, planning for life beyond dentistry means taking a long, honest look at your goals, your finances, your energy, and your legacy.

It's about clarity. It's about readiness. And most of all—it's about choice.

So whether you're ten years from retirement or just beginning to wonder what life will look like when the handpiece goes quiet, this chapter is your invitation to think big—and plan accordingly.

What Does Life After Dentistry Look Like?

For some, it's traditional retirement: no more alarm clocks, no more patients, just time to travel, relax, and enjoy life.

For others, it's a pivot to something new: consulting, teaching, writing, volunteering, or starting a business.

And for many, it's a phased exit: reducing clinical hours, bringing on an associate, or selling part of the practice.

There's no one right answer. But there is one essential truth: if you don't plan for it, it'll be planned for you.

Action Step: Start by asking: If I didn't have to work anymore, how would I spend my time? What would bring me joy, meaning, or purpose?

The Financial Foundation for Retirement Readiness

Before you can plan your lifestyle after dentistry, you need to make sure your financial house is in order.

This means:

- Knowing your retirement number
- Understanding your income sources
- Having a withdrawal strategy
- Planning for healthcare costs
- Reducing debt and simplifying your finances

Retirement Number: How much do you need to live the lifestyle you want, indefinitely?

To calculate this:

- Estimate annual expenses in retirement
- Subtract expected income (Social Security, pensions, rental income)
- Multiply the shortfall by 25 (assuming a 4% safe withdrawal rate)

Example: If you need $120,000/year and expect $40,000 from other sources, you'll need a portfolio of roughly $2 million.

Action Step: Meet with a financial planner to build a retirement income plan—one that includes taxes, inflation, and market volatility.

Transitioning Out of the Practice

Your dental practice may be your largest asset—and your biggest planning challenge.

Options:

- Sell to a corporate dental group
- Sell to an associate
- Merge with another practice
- Wind down over time

Each option has different financial, tax, and emotional implications.

Pros of Selling to Corporate:

- Faster transaction
- Often higher initial offer
- Less involvement post-sale

Cons:

- Less control over practice culture
- May not align with your values or team needs

Pros of Selling to Associate:

- Smoother cultural transition
- Keeps legacy intact
- May allow phased retirement

Cons:

- May require seller financing
- Slower process
- Potential for conflict if not clearly structured

Action Step: Get a valuation from a professional dental transition consultant. Understand the timeline, terms, and tax impact of a sale.

Emotional and Identity Considerations

Dentistry isn't just a job—it's a calling. So walking away from it can feel disorienting.

You might ask:

- Who am I without my title?
- What will my days look like?
- Will I still have purpose, influence, or connection?

These are real questions. Don't brush them off.

Action Step: Begin cultivating other parts of your identity now. Hobbies, friendships, community involvement—don't wait for retirement to build your life.

Healthcare After Dentistry

One of the biggest expenses in retirement is healthcare—especially if you retire before Medicare eligibility at age 65.

Options:

- COBRA (temporary, expensive)
- ACA marketplace plans
- Health-sharing ministries (limited coverage)
- Spouse's employer plan

Also consider:

- Long-term care insurance or alternative strategies
- HSA (health savings account) if available before retirement

Action Step: Build a healthcare plan for ages 60–65, then transition to a Medicare strategy with a trusted advisor.

Real Estate and Lifestyle Downsizing

Many dentists reassess their housing needs in retirement:

- Do you want to downsize?
- Move to a different city or climate?

- Live closer to family?

Also consider real estate as a source of passive income:

- Rental properties
- Selling a second home
- House hacking (renting out part of your home)

Pros of Downsizing:

- Lower expenses and upkeep
- Simplified lifestyle

Cons:

- Emotional attachment
- Moving costs

Action Step: Tour 2–3 neighborhoods where you might want to live in retirement. Start imagining the next chapter.

Designing Your Schedule and Structure

Retirement isn't just about money—it's about how you spend your time. Consider:

- Volunteer opportunities
- Travel and cultural experiences
- Mentoring younger dentists
- Part-time teaching or consulting
- Learning new skills or hobbies

Action Step: Create a sample weekly schedule for your ideal retirement. Include balance between rest, connection, contribution, and fun.

Giving Back and Leaving a Legacy

As you exit your career, you may feel called to contribute in new ways:

- Donating to causes you care about
- Funding scholarships or mission work
- Mentoring or teaching younger professionals
- Creating a charitable trust or foundation

Legacy is about more than wealth—it's about wisdom, values, and impact.

Action Step: Write a legacy letter or video message to your family. Share your hopes, lessons, and what matters most to you.

Common Pitfalls in Dental Retirement

Avoid these missteps:

- Waiting too long to start planning
- Overestimating practice sale proceeds
- Underestimating healthcare costs
- Neglecting emotional prep
- Assuming retirement = never working again

Action Step: Block off time each quarter to review your retirement readiness. Make it a regular part of your financial routine.

Social Security, Pensions, and Other Income Sources

When to take Social Security is a big question.

Basics:

- Eligible at 62, but full benefits at 66–67
- Delaying until 70 = highest monthly payout

Coordinate Social Security with:

- Pension income (if any)
- Retirement account withdrawals
- Spouse's benefits

Also consider:

- Selling appreciated stock or real estate
- Business or consulting income
- Rental income streams

Action Step: Run multiple retirement income scenarios with your advisor. Optimize for taxes, sequence of withdrawals, and risk.

Staying Mentally and Physically Engaged

The happiest retirees stay:

- Socially connected
- Physically active
- Mentally stimulated
- Emotionally purposeful

That doesn't happen by accident—it happens by design.

Ideas:

- Join a club or mastermind group
- Travel with purpose (study tours, faith-based trips)
- Take classes or teach them
- Schedule regular family or grandparent time

Action Step: Make a list of five things you've always wanted to do—but never had time for. Begin exploring them now.

Having "The Talk" With Your Family

As you plan your exit, bring your loved ones into the loop:

- Let your spouse or partner know your vision
- Talk with kids about estate and financial plans
- Share your healthcare wishes and who to call for what

Action Step: Schedule a family meeting. It doesn't have to be formal—just intentional. Use it to share plans, hopes, and logistics.

Closing Thoughts: The Next Chapter Is Yours to Write

You've built something remarkable.

You've cared for people. You've solved problems. You've worked hard—really hard—to get where you are.

And now, it's time to think about what's next.

Not just an end—but a new beginning.

Planning for life beyond dentistry isn't about giving up who you are—it's about expanding who you're becoming. It's about creating space for joy, rest, and meaning. It's about designing a life that fits the person you've become and the dreams you still have.

So don't put it off. Start small. Start today.

Because the future you want won't just show up. You have to build it.

Chapter 14: Exit Strategies for Practice Owners

Let's talk about the end game.

If you own a dental practice, one of the most important decisions you'll ever make isn't about clinical care or staffing. It's about your exit. Because eventually, the day will come when you hang up your white coat—and how you prepare for that moment will determine the financial and emotional return on everything you've built.

And here's the thing: most dentists wait too long to think about it. Or they get overwhelmed. Or they assume it'll somehow work itself out.

But a dental practice isn't just a job. It's an asset. And your exit strategy is the blueprint for how that asset gets converted into time, freedom, and opportunity.

So whether you're five years out or twenty, whether you plan to sell to a DSO, an associate, a friend, or wind down entirely—this chapter will walk you through the real steps, options, and decisions that shape a successful exit.

Let's make sure you leave on your terms—with confidence, clarity, and cash flow.

Start With the End in Mind

Planning your exit isn't about quitting. It's about designing a transition.

Ask yourself:

- When do I want to stop practicing clinically?

- Do I want to stay involved in the business side?
- Who do I want to take over—an individual or a company?
- What do I want my life to look like after the sale?

Action Step: Write out your ideal exit timeline. Include target retirement age, desired lifestyle, and what you hope to do next.

Know the Value of Your Practice

Your practice isn't just worth what you think—it's worth what someone is willing to pay. And that depends on:

- Revenue and profitability
- Patient base and retention
- Location and competition
- Equipment, tech, and facilities
- Staff and systems

The most common method for valuation is a multiple of **EBITDA** (earnings before interest, taxes, depreciation, and amortization).

Action Step: Hire a professional dental transition specialist or CPA to conduct a valuation at least 3–5 years before your target exit.

Understand Your Exit Options

There are several ways to exit your practice. Each comes with its own pros, cons, and timelines.

1. **Sell to a DSO (Dental Support Organization)**
2. **Sell to an Associate or Junior Dentist**
3. **Merge with Another Practice**
4. **Bring on a Partner and Phase Out**
5. **Close the Practice and Liquidate**

Let's walk through each.

1. Selling to a DSO

DSOs have become a popular exit route because they offer:

- Higher initial cash payouts
- Quick timelines
- Operational support and exit paths

Pros:

- Often higher valuation
- Reduced administrative burden
- May allow phased exit (stay on as clinical director)

Cons:

- May feel impersonal or corporate
- Less control over staff retention and patient experience
- Potential earn-outs based on performance

Real-World Example: Dr. Smith sold his two-location practice to a DSO for 6x EBITDA. He stayed on for two years, then fully exited with a second payout. The key was having clean books and a high-margin operation.

1. Selling to an Associate

This is the most personal option—but also the most complex.
Pros:

- Continuity of care for patients
- Legacy stays intact
- Often more flexible terms

Cons:

- Requires mentoring and grooming
- Financing may be more difficult
- Emotional dynamics can complicate the transition

Action Step: If this is your path, start grooming an associate 3–5 years in advance. Create a roadmap to ownership.

1. Merging with Another Practice

Sometimes, merging with a peer can be more lucrative than selling outright.
Pros:

- Shared overhead
- Increased buying power
- Easier future sale as a larger group

Cons:

- Requires shared vision and strong agreement
- Can be messy if goals diverge

Action Step: Look for local practices with complementary strengths. Begin informal conversations well before your planned exit.

1. Bring on a Partner, Then Phase Out

This strategy allows you to reduce your workload over time while maintaining income.
Pros:

- Smooth transition
- Ongoing income stream
- Opportunity to mentor

Cons:

- Slower exit
- Requires clear roles and expectations
- Possible power struggles if not aligned

Action Step: Draft a formal partnership agreement with buy-out terms and a transition timeline.

1. Close and Liquidate

Not ideal, but sometimes necessary—especially for smaller or declining practices.

Pros:

- Simple, clean break
- No ongoing responsibility

Cons:

- Minimal financial return
- Patient abandonment risk if not handled well

Action Step: Consult legal counsel about required notifications and steps for closing a practice ethically.

Prepare Financially for the Transition

Your exit should fund your future—not just close a chapter.

You need to plan for:

- Taxes on the sale (capital gains, ordinary income)
- Investment strategy for the proceeds
- Healthcare and insurance coverage
- Estate planning updates

Action Step: Meet with a financial planner and tax advisor 1–2 years before your exit to model your net after-tax proceeds and plan your portfolio reallocation.

Clean Up Before You Sell

Buyers don't want a mess. Before listing your practice or beginning conversations:

- Streamline your accounts receivable
- Improve hygiene recall and case acceptance rates
- Update outdated equipment if ROI makes sense
- Document systems and staff roles
- Review lease terms or real estate ownership

Action Step: Create a due diligence checklist. Start ticking things off now so you're ready when opportunity comes.

Navigating the Emotional Side of the Exit

This is real—and it's big.

You may feel:

- Excitement and relief
- Loss of purpose or identity
- Grief or nostalgia
- Anxiety about "what's next"

This is normal. You're not alone.

Action Step: Start envisioning your next chapter—whether it's consulting, teaching, traveling, or volunteering. Don't retire into a void. Retire into something new.

Practice Sale Timeline: A 5-Year Countdown

5 Years Out:

- Get a valuation
- Talk to advisors

- Explore exit options
- Begin grooming successors (if applicable)

3 Years Out:

- Optimize operations and profitability
- Reduce unnecessary expenses
- Tighten systems and staffing
- Clean up documentation

2 Years Out:

- Choose your path (DSO, associate, merge)
- Begin formal negotiations or preparations
- Secure your personal financial plan

1 Year Out:

- Finalize sale terms
- Communicate with team and patients
- Update estate and financial documents

Post-Sale:

- Transition smoothly (if staying on)
- Celebrate your career
- Launch into your next chapter

Closing Thoughts: Leave on Your Terms

You've poured your life into your practice.

You've built relationships, created jobs, cared for patients, and served your community.

You deserve an exit that reflects all that.

So start planning now.

Not out of fear—but out of respect.

Respect for what you've built. And for the life you still have ahead.

Your next chapter isn't just about stepping away. It's about stepping into something new.

You've got this.

And when the time comes—you'll be ready.

Chapter 15: Staying Engaged Without Burning Out

Let's start with a feeling you probably know all too well.

You wake up, already exhausted. You gear up for another packed day—patients, procedures, staffing issues, bills, insurance drama, maybe a lunch that's really just catching up on paperwork. You go home, crash, wake up, repeat. Some days are fine. Others feel like a weight is pressing down on your chest.

You might love what you do—but you're also tired.

This chapter is for every dentist who wants to keep going without losing themselves along the way. For the young associate trying to prove their worth. For the mid-career owner who hasn't taken a real vacation in years. For the practice leader silently wondering if burnout is just part of the job.

It's not.

This chapter is about creating a sustainable, meaningful career in dentistry—one that supports your mental health, honors your values, and keeps you financially strong without sacrificing everything else.

Let's talk about how to stay engaged without burning out.

Understanding Burnout in Dentistry

Burnout isn't just being tired. It's chronic emotional and physical exhaustion, often paired with cynicism and a sense of inefficacy. It happens when:

- You care deeply, but feel like it's never enough

- You work hard, but the reward feels hollow
- You're always "on," but never fully present

Burnout isn't a weakness—it's a warning sign.

And in dentistry, it's especially common due to:

- Physical strain and repetitive movements
- Emotional labor of patient care
- Business management pressures
- Financial stress (student debt, overhead, insurance)
- Isolation (many practice owners feel alone at the top)

Action Step: Ask yourself honestly—how's your energy? Are you running on fumes? Are you still excited—or just enduring?

The Cost of Burning Out

Burnout isn't just a feeling. It affects:

- Your clinical decision-making
- Your relationships with staff and patients
- Your physical health (back pain, headaches, immune issues)
- Your finances (missed work, lower productivity)
- Your sense of purpose and identity

Some dentists burn out so completely they:

- Leave the profession altogether
- Sell too early or too cheap
- Withdraw from family and friends
- Lose joy in the parts of life that used to recharge them

Let's not let it get there.

Redefining Success On Your Terms

The first step to staying engaged is redefining what success looks like—on your terms.

It's easy to get caught in the trap:

- Bigger practice = success
- More procedures = success
- More revenue = success

But what if success meant:

- Being present with your family
- Taking two real vacations a year
- Running a profitable, low-stress practice
- Having time to exercise, sleep, and breathe

Action Step: Write your own success statement. Not someone else's definition. Yours.

Setting Boundaries Without Guilt

You are allowed to say no.

To extra hours. To difficult patients. To toxic staff behavior. To weekend emergencies that could wait until Monday.

Setting boundaries isn't selfish—it's sustainable.

Boundaries to consider:

- Office hours you truly honor
- Days you don't check email
- Time blocks for family or self-care
- Limits on how many high-stress procedures you take on weekly

Action Step: Choose one boundary to implement this month. Communicate it clearly. Honor it fiercely.

Designing a Sustainable Schedule

The traditional dental week is grueling—four or five packed clinical days, followed by administrative catch-up.

What if you:

- Compressed your schedule to four days?
- Saw fewer patients, but increased production per visit?
- Blocked admin time into your week?
- Took one mental health day each quarter?

Less hustle. More intention.

Action Step: Audit your current schedule. What's draining you? Where's the wiggle room?

Delegating, Outsourcing, and Trusting Your Team

You don't have to do everything.

You are not the only one who can:

- Order supplies
- Train new staff
- Manage the hygiene schedule
- Handle insurance calls

Empower your team. Outsource what you can. Protect your clinical energy for the work only you can do.

Action Step: Make a list of everything you do in a week. Circle three things someone else could take on. Delegate one this week.

Managing the Business Without Losing Yourself

Being a business owner and a clinician is a lot. It's two jobs.

Strategies to reduce business overwhelm:

- Hire a great office manager with decision-making authority
- Work with a dental-specific CPA and financial advisor
- Use dashboards to track metrics instead of micromanaging
- Meet monthly with your leadership team instead of daily firefighting

Action Step: Schedule a monthly leadership meeting. Set a rhythm. Make it about alignment—not stress.

Protecting Your Physical Health

Burnout isn't just mental. It shows up in your body.

Take care of:

- Your posture (ergonomic chairs, loupes, stretching routines)
- Your sleep (a non-negotiable foundation)
- Your nutrition (skip the sugar-crash lunches)
- Your movement (walk, lift, stretch—just move)

Action Step: Book a physical therapy or posture consult. Prevent small issues from becoming career-threatening.

Managing Mental and Emotional Wellness

You don't have to carry it all alone.

Ways to care for your mental health:

- Therapy or coaching
- Peer support or mastermind groups
- Journaling or meditation
- Setting emotional boundaries with patients and staff

Signs you may need more support:

- Irritability or numbness
- Avoiding the office
- Trouble sleeping or concentrating
- Feeling detached from your work or loved ones

Action Step: Schedule a therapy session or talk to a coach—before things feel unmanageable.

Using Money as a Tool to Buy Back Time and Peace

Financial freedom isn't just about early retirement. It's about reducing pressure *now*.

Use money to:

- Hire more help
- Work fewer days
- Take breaks without guilt
- Invest in systems and staff training

Action Step: Identify one way your money could buy you time or sanity. Spend intentionally on that this month.

Investing in Your Own Growth

Burnout sometimes masks boredom.

Stay engaged by learning:

- New procedures that excite you
- New leadership or business skills
- Personal interests outside of dentistry

You're allowed to grow beyond your drill.

Action Step: Sign up for one course, CE, or retreat that inspires you—something just for you.

Real-Life Stories: Dentists Who Reclaimed Their Joy

Dr. A was on the brink of selling her practice from burnout. She took a sabbatical, restructured her schedule, delegated operations—and fell back in love with dentistry.

Dr. B was seeing 40 patients a day and falling apart. He hired an associate, cut down to three days, and used the time to mentor young dentists.

Dr. C didn't change her hours—but she started meditating, journaling, and seeing a therapist. The work was the same—but she was different.

Rewriting the Narrative of a Dental Career

This isn't just about you.

It's about the culture of dentistry—the one that tells us to grind, hustle, smile through the pain, and pretend it's all fine.

Let's write a new story:

- One where success includes rest
- Where leadership means vulnerability
- Where sustainability beats burnout
- Where you can have a profitable, meaningful practice—and a life

Closing Thoughts: You're Not a Machine. You're a Human.

You became a dentist to help people. But you're a person, too.

You deserve support. You deserve rest. You deserve a career that gives back to you—not just one you give to.

Staying engaged isn't about trying harder. It's about working smarter, setting boundaries, finding joy, and remembering that you matter.

You're not alone in this. And you don't have to burn out to succeed.

You've got this. Let's build something sustainable. Together.

Chapter 16: Choosing the Right Financial Advisor

Let's begin with a simple truth:

Dentistry is a full-time profession. Financial planning shouldn't have to be.

As a dentist, you're trained to diagnose, to treat, to lead a team, and to run a business. But navigating complex financial decisions—investments, taxes, retirement planning, insurance strategies, practice transitions—that's an entirely different world.

And that's exactly why having the *right* financial advisor can make all the difference.

This chapter is here to help you understand who to trust, what to look for, what red flags to avoid, and how to build a relationship with a financial professional that supports your goals, respects your values, and gives you confidence in your future.

Whether you're just starting out or you're a seasoned practice owner ready for succession planning, choosing the right advisor is one of the most important financial decisions you'll make.

Let's do it wisely.

Why Dentists Need Specialized Financial Advice

Dentists face a unique blend of financial complexity:

- High student debt
- High earning potential

- Practice ownership
- Real estate decisions
- Tax strategy
- Family and lifestyle planning
- Asset protection

This is not a one-size-fits-all situation.

A good advisor for a dentist must understand:

- The structure of dental practices
- The pros and cons of S-corporations
- How to structure retirement plans for business owners
- Insurance needs unique to clinicians
- Succession and exit planning

If your advisor doesn't understand dentistry, they're guessing. And guessing isn't a financial strategy.

Action Step: Make a list of the financial areas where you feel least confident. These are the areas where a good advisor should step in and bring clarity.

What Does a Financial Advisor Actually Do?

Let's demystify the job.

A real financial advisor helps you:

- Clarify your goals
- Build a long-term plan
- Select appropriate investment strategies
- Reduce taxes
- Structure your cash flow
- Review insurance and protect your income
- Prepare for major transitions (buying a practice, having kids, selling your business)

A good advisor doesn't just sell products—they coach, guide, and plan with you.

The Different Types of Advisors (and How They Get Paid)

There are several types of financial professionals, and it's important to know the differences:

1. **Fee-Only Fiduciary Advisors**

- Paid directly by you
- Do not earn commissions
- Required to act in your best interest

1. **Fee-Based Advisors**

- Charge a combination of fees and commissions
- May have conflicts of interest (incentivized to recommend certain products)

1. **Commission-Only Advisors or Insurance Agents**

- Paid based on the products they sell
- Often limited in what they can offer

1. **Robo-Advisors**

- Algorithm-driven platforms for investing
- Low-cost, but limited personalization

Action Step: Ask every advisor you meet: "How are you compensated?" and "Are you a fiduciary 100% of the time?"

Understanding the Fiduciary Standard

This one's big.

A **fiduciary** is legally obligated to act in your best interest. Not just to recommend something "suitable," but to choose what's best for *you.*

Not all financial professionals are fiduciaries.

Red Flag: If they dodge this question or say, "Sometimes we act as a fiduciary," that means they *don't* always put you first.

Action Step: Only work with advisors who are fiduciaries 100% of the time. Ask them to put it in writing.

What Credentials Should You Look For?

Not all letters behind someone's name mean the same thing. Here are the ones that count:

- **CFP® (Certified Financial Planner)** – Broad financial planning expertise, strong ethical standards
- **CPA/PFS (Certified Public Accountant / Personal Financial Specialist)** – Excellent for tax and financial planning
- **CFA (Chartered Financial Analyst)** – Deep investment knowledge (more common for portfolio managers)

Less useful or potentially sales-focused:

- CLU, ChFC, LUTCF (often insurance designations)

Action Step: Ask, "What credentials do you hold, and how do they help you serve dentists specifically?"

The Traits of a Great Dental-Specific Advisor

Beyond the licenses and designations, the *right* advisor for you should:

- Understand the dental world—insurance, overhead, practice value, etc.
- Have experience with clients like you (dentists, specialists, practice owners)
- Be proactive, not reactive
- Explain things clearly without jargon
- Help with goal-setting, not just investments
- Work well with your CPA, attorney, and team

Red Flag: If you leave every meeting confused or unsure about what they're doing for you—it's a problem.

The Process: What a Great Advisor Relationship Should Look Like

Here's what a real advisor does—not just in year one, but every year:

Year One:

- Discovery meeting (goals, values, history)
- Review of current financial situation
- Creation of a personalized financial plan
- Coordination with CPA and attorney
- Investment strategy implementation
- Insurance review
- Ongoing communication plan

Ongoing Years:

- Annual plan updates
- Tax planning before year-end
- Portfolio review and rebalancing
- Big-picture check-ins (new goals, life changes)
- Practice transition or retirement prep

Action Step: Ask the advisor, "What does your process look like in the first 12 months? What can I expect?"

Real Questions to Ask a Potential Advisor

When interviewing an advisor, don't just listen to the pitch. Ask:

- Who do you specialize in working with?
- Are you a fiduciary 100% of the time?
- How do you get paid?
- What's your process for building a plan?
- What happens if I want to leave?
- Can I see a sample financial plan (with personal info removed)?

- How often will we meet?
- Will you coordinate with my CPA or estate attorney?
- How do you help clients during downturns or volatility?

Action Step: Interview at least two advisors. Don't rush it. You're building a relationship, not hiring a product.

Common Red Flags to Avoid

- Pressure to buy insurance or investment products early in the relationship
- Lack of a clear planning process
- Over-promising returns or focusing too much on performance
- Vague about fees or commissions
- Doesn't understand your practice structure or dental career path

Action Step: Trust your gut. If something feels off—it probably is.

Should You Work With a Local Advisor?

Not necessarily. Today, many top advisors serve clients virtually. What matters more than geography is:

- Expertise with dentists
- Communication and availability
- Fit with your personality and goals

That said, some people value the ability to meet in person. If that's important to you, make it part of your criteria.

Understanding the Cost—and the Value

Typical advisory fees:

- 1% of assets under management (AUM), often with tiered reductions at higher levels
- Flat fees ($3,000–$10,000/year depending on complexity)
- Hourly planning ($200–$500/hour)

What you're paying for:

- Peace of mind
- Integrated strategy
- Coordination with other professionals
- Tax savings opportunities
- Accountability and behavioral guidance

A great advisor *more than pays for themselves* through tax strategy, risk mitigation, and smart decision-making.

How to End an Unproductive Advisor Relationship

If your advisor isn't helping—or if you feel dismissed or confused—it's okay to move on.

Steps:

- Request a transfer of assets (your new advisor can help)
- Review any termination clauses or fees
- Inform your advisor respectfully
- Reflect on what you want differently this time

Action Step: If you've been putting off a change, set a deadline to make a decision. This is your financial life—you get to choose.

Real-Life Story: A Practice Owner's Advisor Upgrade

Dr. Maria had a nice practice and a "financial guy" she'd worked with for years. But she always felt like she was being sold something.

When she hired a dental-specific CFP®, she finally got a full plan: student loan strategy, tax-efficient investing, disability coverage that made sense, and a clear 10-year roadmap. That advisor became her go-to partner through a practice expansion and eventual buy-out.

It changed everything.

Closing Thoughts: You Deserve Great Advice

You've worked too hard—and sacrificed too much—to go it alone financially.

You deserve a professional who listens, guides, and helps you turn your income into real wealth.

Choosing the right advisor isn't just about money. It's about clarity. Confidence. And knowing someone's got your back as life—and business—get more complex.

So ask the questions. Take your time. Trust your gut.

And remember: the right advisor doesn't talk down to you or talk over you. They walk *with* you.

You've got this. Let's build a team that helps you thrive.

Chapter 17: Working With a CPA Who Understands Dentistry

Let's start with a truth most dentists learn the hard way:

Not all CPAs are created equal.

Sure, any certified public accountant can file your taxes. But when it comes to understanding the unique financial challenges, opportunities, and structures that come with being a dentist—especially a practice owner—having a CPA who *really gets it* can make the difference between just getting by and building something great.

This chapter is about helping you find that CPA. The one who doesn't just prepare your returns but partners with you in planning your future. The one who understands your industry, anticipates what's coming, and helps you make smarter, more strategic decisions—all while keeping more money in your pocket.

Whether you're just starting your dental career or leading a multi-location practice, this is your guide to choosing, working with, and fully leveraging a CPA who understands dentistry.

Why Dentists Need a Specialized CPA

Dentists face a unique financial landscape:

- High student debt
- High-income potential
- Practice ownership with complicated tax implications
- Equipment depreciation and Section 179 planning

- Complex entity structures (LLCs, S-Corps)
- Retirement plan optimization
- Real estate investments tied to the practice

This isn't something you want a generalist learning on your dime.

Action Step: Ask yourself—does my current CPA know the top three tax strategies specific to dentists? If not, it may be time for a change.

What Should a Dental-Specific CPA Help With?

A great dental CPA does more than file your taxes. They:

- Analyze overhead and profitability
- Help select and optimize your business structure
- Plan for retirement contributions and deductions
- Monitor equipment depreciation schedules
- Guide Section 179 and bonus depreciation usage
- Coordinate with your financial advisor
- Advise on tax-efficient compensation strategies
- Help manage associate pay and contractor classification
- Provide transition planning for buying or selling a practice

Real-World Example: Dr. Taylor switched to a dental CPA who identified an opportunity to reclassify $100,000 of expenses and save $28,000 in taxes that year. Same numbers, smarter eyes.

Understanding Your Business Entity

Your business entity affects how you're taxed, paid, and protected.

Common choices for dentists:

- Sole Proprietorship
- LLC (Limited Liability Company)
- S-Corporation (S-Corp)
- C-Corporation (less common for dentists)

Most common: LLC taxed as an S-Corp

Why? It allows you to:

- Take a reasonable salary
- Distribute remaining profits as dividends (not subject to self-employment tax)
- Deduct more business expenses legally

Action Step: Ask your CPA to review your entity structure annually. As your income or business size grows, your structure may need to evolve.

Key Tax Strategies for Dentists

Here are some tax strategies your CPA should bring to the table:

1. **Section 179 Expensing:** Deduct up to $1 million in qualifying equipment purchases each year.
2. **Bonus Depreciation:** Accelerated write-offs for large capital investments.
3. **Retirement Plan Contributions:** Maximize contributions to Solo 401(k), SEP IRA, or Defined Benefit Plans.
4. **S-Corp Salary Optimization:** Balance salary and distributions for tax efficiency.
5. **Home Office Deduction (if you work remotely):** Deduct a portion of home utilities, mortgage, internet, etc.
6. **Business Auto Deduction:** Track mileage or actual vehicle expenses for tax deductions.
7. **Family Employee Strategy:** Hire your kids for legitimate work and deduct their wages (limits apply).

Action Step: Have a pre-year-end tax planning meeting (usually October or November) to project your tax liability and adjust strategies before December 31st.

Tax Planning vs. Tax Preparation

Let's get clear:

- **Tax preparation** is filing your return.
- **Tax planning** is designing your strategy to minimize what you owe.

Too many dentists only get tax prep.

A great CPA does both.

They look forward—not just backward.

Action Step: Ask your CPA: "How do you help me plan proactively for tax savings—not just report after the fact?"

What Reports Should Your CPA Provide?

You deserve visibility into your financial life. Ask for:

- Profit and Loss Statement (monthly and YTD)
- Balance Sheet
- Cash Flow Statement
- Overhead Analysis (total and by category)
- Break-even Analysis
- Tax Projection Summary (quarterly)

These reports help you make smart business decisions—not just react to tax bills.

Action Step: Schedule a quarterly review with your CPA to go over key numbers. Don't just meet once a year.

Working With Your CPA as a Team Player

Your CPA should coordinate with:

- Your financial advisor
- Your attorney (especially for estate or practice transitions)
- Your office manager or bookkeeper

The best CPAs aren't just math people—they're communication people.

Action Step: Introduce your CPA to your advisor. A great team works together to support *your* goals.

Questions to Ask When Interviewing a CPA

When looking for a dental CPA, ask:

- How many dental clients do you work with?
- What's your experience with practice transitions?
- Do you work with practice brokers, bankers, or DSOs?
- How do you bill—flat fee or hourly?
- How often will we meet or communicate?
- Can you help with overhead and profitability, not just taxes?
- Do you offer proactive tax planning?
- What do you need from me to do your best work?

Action Step: Interview at least two CPAs. Ask real questions. Listen not just to the answers—but how they explain them.

When It Might Be Time to Switch CPAs

If your current CPA:

- Only talks to you in April
- Doesn't understand your practice structure
- Misses deductions or tax-saving strategies
- Leaves you confused after every meeting
- Is slow to respond or dismissive of questions

It's okay to move on.

Action Step: If switching is on your mind, set a deadline to make a decision. Loyalty is nice—but not when it costs you money or peace of mind.

Real-World Stories From the Chair

Dr. Shah had used the same CPA for 12 years. After a colleague's recommendation, she switched to a dental-specific CPA who restructured her compensation model, added a defined benefit plan, and reduced her annual tax bill by over $40,000.

Dr. Lewis was nervous to switch but found that his new CPA helped him prepare his practice for sale, guided the valuation process, and helped him net $150,000 more than he expected in his exit.

Sometimes the right CPA isn't just about taxes. It's about *strategy.*

Closing Thoughts: You Deserve More Than Just a Tax Preparer

You've worked too hard, sacrificed too much, and built something too important to work with a CPA who doesn't understand your world.

The right CPA doesn't just reduce your tax bill. They reduce your stress.

They help you:

- See clearly
- Plan strategically
- Spend wisely
- Grow intentionally

So don't settle. Ask better questions. Interview new options. Expect more from your CPA—because you deserve it.

You've got this. Let's make sure your numbers work for *you.*

Chapter 18: Finding the Right Estate Planning Attorney

Let's start with a deep breath and a reminder: this isn't about doom and gloom. It's about peace and preparation.

As a dentist, you've spent your life helping people. You've built a practice, earned your income, supported your family, and made a difference in the lives of your patients and your community. But one day—whether far down the road or much sooner than expected—you won't be here to manage it all.

And that's why estate planning matters.

This chapter is about more than just wills and legal documents. It's about choosing the right estate planning attorney who can help you organize, protect, and pass on everything you've built. Someone who can take complex ideas—asset protection, trusts, tax mitigation, guardianship—and make them clear, manageable, and personalized for your life.

Whether you're early in your dental career or already thinking about your legacy, this chapter is your guide to finding a legal partner who understands what you've worked so hard to create—and helps you pass it on the right way.

Let's talk about how to choose the right estate planning attorney for your journey.

Why Dentists Need a Strong Estate Plan

As a dentist, you may:

- Own a valuable practice
- Have a high income or large retirement savings
- Hold real estate tied to your business
- Have children or dependents
- Want to minimize estate taxes
- Need to protect assets from liability

Estate planning helps ensure:

- Your loved ones are cared for
- Your assets go where you want them to
- Your practice can transition smoothly
- Your tax burden is minimized
- Your wishes are honored during illness or incapacity

Action Step: Ask yourself—if something happened to me tomorrow, would my family and team know what to do next? If not, it's time to start.

What an Estate Planning Attorney Does (And Why You Need One)

A great estate planning attorney doesn't just draft documents. They help you:

- Clarify your goals and wishes
- Evaluate what you own and how it's structured
- Protect your family, heirs, and business
- Create plans for healthcare and decision-making if you're incapacitated
- Ensure everything is legally sound and tax-efficient

They can:

- Draft wills and trusts
- Create healthcare directives and powers of attorney
- Design complex trust structures for high-net-worth individuals
- Help structure practice transitions or business continuity plans

- Coordinate with your CPA and financial advisor

Action Step: Write down the top three goals you'd want an estate plan to accomplish. Bring these to your first meeting with a prospective attorney.

Traits of a Great Estate Planning Attorney (for Dentists)

You're not just looking for a lawyer. You're looking for:

- A good listener who understands your values
- A clear communicator who explains without legal jargon
- A strategic thinker who considers taxes, business, and family dynamics
- A collaborator who will coordinate with your financial and tax professionals
- Someone with experience working with healthcare professionals or practice owners

Bonus: A great estate planning attorney often asks questions you didn't know to ask—and helps you think long-term.

What Legal Documents Should You Have?

Every dentist's situation is unique, but common documents include:

- **Last Will and Testament:** Outlines asset distribution and guardianship
- **Revocable Living Trust:** Avoids probate and provides more control
- **Durable Power of Attorney:** Designates someone to handle your finances if you're incapacitated
- **Healthcare Proxy / Medical Power of Attorney:** Names someone to make medical decisions for you
- **Living Will / Advance Directive:** States your end-of-life care preferences
- **HIPAA Release Form:** Allows someone to access your medical information
- **Practice Succession Plan or Buy-Sell Agreement:** Outlines what happens to your business

Action Step: Review this list and identify any documents you don't yet have. These are the first things to bring up with your attorney.

Trusts vs. Wills: What's the Difference?

Wills:

- Public document
- Goes through probate
- Can be contested
- Simpler to draft, but slower to execute

Trusts:

- Private document
- Avoids probate (saves time, money)
- Allows for conditions (e.g., kids get money at age 30)
- Can include asset protection features

For many dentists: A combination of both makes sense.

Action Step: Ask your attorney, "Would a revocable living trust make sense given my net worth, practice, and goals?"

Estate Planning Mistakes to Avoid

1. **Putting it off too long**
2. **Only doing a will and ignoring incapacity planning**
3. **Failing to update documents after life changes**
4. **Not aligning financial accounts with your plan**
5. **Forgetting about digital assets**
6. **Not discussing your plan with your family**

Real-World Story: Dr. Kim created a will years ago but never updated her retirement account beneficiaries after her divorce. Her ex-spouse received a six-figure distribution. A quick review could've avoided the mistake.

Action Step: Review all your accounts and insurance policies. Make sure your beneficiaries are up to date—and aligned with your estate plan.

Questions to Ask When Interviewing an Estate Planning Attorney

- How long have you been practicing estate law?
- How many dentists or business owners do you serve?
- Do you handle both simple and complex planning?
- Will you coordinate with my financial planner and CPA?
- Do you charge a flat fee or hourly?
- How often should I review or update my plan?
- What's your process for creating and implementing a plan?

Action Step: Schedule free consultations with at least two estate planning attorneys. Take notes and compare their approach.

How Often Should You Update Your Estate Plan?

Update your plan when you:

- Get married or divorced
- Have a child (or a child turns 18)
- Move to a new state
- Open or sell a practice
- Receive a large inheritance
- Have a major change in health or family dynamics
- Experience a significant increase in net worth

Rule of Thumb: Review your plan every 3–5 years or after any major life event.

Action Step: Add a recurring reminder on your calendar to review your plan every three years.

Digital Assets and Your Estate Plan

More and more of your life lives online:

- Bank accounts
- Social media

- Practice management software
- Email and cloud storage
- Cryptocurrency

A good estate plan includes:

- An inventory of digital assets
- A secure password plan
- Clear instructions on who can access what

Action Step: Create a digital access list. Store it securely and update it annually.

Your Practice Is Part of Your Estate

Your dental practice may be:

- An active business you plan to sell
- A partnership with buy-sell provisions
- A legacy business you want to pass down

Your estate planning attorney should:

- Review your practice ownership documents
- Coordinate with your CPA and practice transition consultant
- Help create a succession plan or sale timeline

Action Step: Ask your attorney, "How would my practice be handled if something happened to me tomorrow?"

Integrating Estate Planning With Your Financial Plan

Your estate plan shouldn't sit on a shelf. It should be part of your broader financial strategy.

That means:

- Coordinating with your CPA (for tax impact)

- Working with your financial advisor (on titling and funding trusts)
- Including insurance strategies (to provide liquidity or equalize inheritance)

Action Step: Host a joint meeting (virtual or in-person) with your attorney, advisor, and CPA to ensure everyone's on the same page.

Closing Thoughts: This Is About Peace, Not Paperwork

Estate planning can feel heavy. But at its heart, it's a gift.

It's a gift of clarity for your family. A gift of time and simplicity for those you love. A gift of protection for your business and your team.

So don't wait. Don't wing it. Don't settle for a fill-in-the-blank will and hope for the best.

Find the right estate planning attorney. Someone who listens. Someone who explains. Someone who cares.

Because you deserve peace of mind. And your legacy deserves a plan.

You've got this. Let's protect what you've built—and pass it on with intention.

Chapter 19: When You Need a Business Attorney

Let's start with a simple truth:

Running a dental practice isn't just about clinical excellence. It's a business.

And like any business, there will be moments when you need legal expertise—not just to get out of trouble, but to avoid it in the first place. This chapter is about knowing when that moment is. It's about understanding the role a business attorney plays in your journey as a dental professional, and why having one on your team is a proactive, protective, and powerful move.

Whether you're starting a new practice, growing a multi-location operation, managing associates, or selling your business, a skilled business attorney can help you make smarter decisions, avoid costly missteps, and keep your practice—and your peace of mind—intact.

Let's talk about when, why, and how to work with a business attorney who understands the dental world.

Why a Dentist Needs a Business Attorney

Most dentists don't think about attorneys until something goes wrong:

- A contract dispute
- A lawsuit threat
- A deal gone sour

But a great business attorney isn't just a firefighter—they're a strategic advisor. They help you:

- Understand your legal exposure
- Draft clear contracts and agreements
- Navigate regulatory compliance
- Structure your business properly
- Protect intellectual property (like your logo or practice name)
- Plan for partnerships, buyouts, or sales

Action Step: Think about the three most legally complex decisions you've made in your dental career. Were you confident in each one—or were you guessing?

What a Business Attorney Actually Does

A business attorney helps with:

- Business formation (LLC, S-Corp, etc.)
- Partnership agreements
- Associate and employee contracts
- Lease negotiation and review
- Vendor agreements
- Employment law compliance
- Practice sales or acquisitions
- Risk mitigation
- Litigation avoidance or response

They're not here to replace your CPA or financial advisor. They're part of your triangle of professional support—each bringing their expertise to your big picture.

Real-World Example: Dr. M partnered with a childhood friend to open a second location. They skipped a formal agreement. Three years later, they had to split—and the lack of clarity cost them over $100,000 in legal fees and lost revenue. A $2,500 attorney's fee at the start could have prevented it all.

When to Hire a Business Attorney

Here are the key moments to bring in legal support:

1. **Starting or Buying a Practice** You'll need help with:

- Entity formation
- Purchase or lease agreements
- Due diligence
- Employment agreements

1. **Bringing on an Associate or Partner**

- Compensation and non-compete clauses
- Buy-in structure
- Exit planning
- Ownership terms

1. **Signing a Lease or Building Contract**

- Reviewing lease language (terms, liabilities, personal guarantees)
- Negotiating fair clauses (renewals, maintenance, subleasing)
- Managing timelines and penalties

1. **Selling or Merging Your Practice**

- Letter of intent (LOI)
- Asset purchase agreement
- Transition plan
- Liability and indemnification language

1. **Dealing with Legal Disputes**

- Employee complaints
- Regulatory investigations
- Contract disagreements

1. **Ongoing Legal Compliance**

- HIPAA
- OSHA
- Employment law

Action Step: Make a checklist of these events. If any are on your horizon, schedule a call with a business attorney *before* you sign anything.

Choosing the Right Attorney for Your Practice

Not every attorney understands dentistry. Look for:

- Experience working with dentists or healthcare businesses
- Familiarity with dental contracts, associateships, and DSOs
- Clear, responsive communication
- Transparent billing practices
- A strategic mindset—not just a legal checklist

Questions to ask:

- What percentage of your clients are healthcare providers?
- Can you walk me through how you'd structure an associate agreement?
- What is your fee structure—flat fee or hourly?
- How do you coordinate with my CPA and financial advisor?

Action Step: Interview at least two attorneys. See who listens, who understands your world, and who earns your trust.

Understanding Legal Fees

Attorneys usually bill in one of three ways:

- **Hourly rate:** You pay for every call, email, and review (typical for ongoing matters)
- **Flat fee:** A single amount for a defined service (contracts, agreements)
- **Retainer:** A monthly fee for ongoing access and priority service (good for growing practices)

Don't be afraid to ask for:

- Flat fee packages for common legal needs
- Clear estimates and billing timelines
- Regular updates so you're not surprised

Action Step: Get your fee agreement in writing. Make sure it outlines what's included and what's extra.

Essential Documents Every Dentist Should Have Reviewed by a Business Attorney

1. **Entity Formation Documents**

- Articles of incorporation
- Operating agreement (if LLC)
- Bylaws (if corporation)

1. **Employment Agreements**

- For associates, hygienists, and staff
- Non-compete and non-solicit clauses
- Compensation and bonus structures

1. **Buy-Sell Agreements**

- Partnership terms
- Exit scenarios

- Valuation method

1. **Lease Agreements**

- Renewal terms
- Landlord responsibilities
- Early exit provisions

1. **Vendor Contracts**

- Equipment purchases
- Lab agreements
- Software licenses

1. **Transition or Sale Agreements**

- Practice valuations
- Purchase terms
- Transition responsibilities

Action Step: Collect these documents from your files. Schedule a document review with your attorney. Fix what's outdated or unclear.

Common Legal Pitfalls Dentists Should Avoid

1. **Using generic contracts from the internet**
2. **Hiring associates without written agreements**
3. **Signing leases without negotiation**
4. **Failing to plan for partner exits**
5. **Merging without a legal transition strategy**
6. **Ignoring regulatory compliance until it's too late**

Action Step: Review your biggest legal vulnerability today. Is it your lease? Your associate contracts? Start there.

Your Business Attorney and the Big Picture

Your business attorney should work with your team:

- CPA: To align tax and entity strategies
- Financial advisor: To plan for transitions and retirement
- Insurance agent: To protect against liability

A good attorney doesn't create silos. They connect dots.

Action Step: Host a joint call with your CPA, advisor, and attorney once a year. Build alignment—and peace of mind.

Litigation vs. Prevention: The Case for Proactive Legal Support

Litigation is expensive, stressful, and time-consuming.

Legal prevention is:

- Clear contracts
- Good documentation
- Staff training
- Systems and SOPs
- Annual checkups

Real-World Story: Dr. T had a team member sue for wrongful termination. Because she had detailed performance documentation, a clear employee handbook, and legal counsel early—the case was dismissed. Her preparation saved her six figures.

Action Step: Schedule an annual legal audit. Just like you review your clinical CE or financial plan—check your legal readiness.

Closing Thoughts: Your Practice Is a Business—Treat It That Way

You didn't become a dentist to become a lawyer.

But you did become a business owner the day you signed your first lease, hired your first team member, or opened your doors.

The right attorney won't just protect your practice—they'll empower it.

They'll help you:

- Make decisions with clarity
- Create agreements that last
- Reduce stress around risk
- Plan for growth, transition, and legacy

So don't wait until something goes wrong. Build your team now. Find a legal partner who listens, teaches, protects, and helps you lead with confidence.

You've got this. And with the right counsel—you're not alone in it.

Chapter 20: Asset Protection for Dentists

Let's get something clear right from the beginning:

If you've worked hard to build wealth—your practice, your savings, your home, your retirement accounts—you deserve to protect it.

And as a dentist, you're in a unique position. You have a high income, a public-facing profession, a business that carries risk, and the real possibility of being the target of a lawsuit—whether fair or frivolous. That combination makes you a prime candidate for thoughtful, proactive asset protection planning.

This chapter isn't about paranoia—it's about prevention. It's about putting the right structures in place so that your wealth stays yours, your family's future is secure, and your peace of mind stays intact, no matter what happens.

Let's walk through the why, when, and how of asset protection—for you, your practice, and everything you've worked for.

What Is Asset Protection?

Asset protection is the strategy of organizing your personal and business assets in a way that shields them from potential creditors, lawsuits, or other claims.

In short: it's about putting up legal walls before someone tries to come through the door.

This includes:

- Legal entity structuring (LLCs, S-Corps, trusts)

- Liability insurance coverage
- Titling assets properly
- Retirement account strategies
- Estate planning tools
- Operating procedures to reduce risk

Action Step: Ask yourself: If someone sued me tomorrow, what could they reach? That's your starting point.

Why Dentists Are High-Risk Targets

You're not just a professional—you're a business owner. And with that comes exposure:

- Malpractice claims (even if you did everything right)
- Slip-and-fall incidents in your office
- Employee lawsuits
- Business disputes with partners, vendors, or landlords
- Personal liability from car accidents or personal guarantees

Real-World Story: Dr. L was in a minor car accident driving to work. The other driver's attorney found out she owned a practice and sued for damages far above the actual harm. Her umbrella insurance saved her. Her practice structure kept her personal accounts safe.

The Golden Rule of Asset Protection

Start *before* you need it.

Once a lawsuit is filed or a claim is pending, courts can invalidate transfers that look like you're trying to hide assets. That's called a fraudulent conveyance.

Asset protection only works when done in advance. It's a fence you build before the storm.

Action Step: Schedule an asset protection check-up with your attorney or financial planner. Don't wait until you're in trouble.

Key Asset Protection Strategies for Dentists

1. **Form the Right Business Entity**

- Use an LLC or S-Corp to separate business from personal liability
- Never operate as a sole proprietor once you own a practice

Pros:

- Protection from business debts and lawsuits
- More control over compensation and taxes

Cons:

- Requires proper setup and maintenance
- Not bulletproof without good procedures

Action Step: Review your entity structure. Is your practice set up correctly—and operating like a real business on paper?

1. **Maximize Liability Insurance**

- Malpractice insurance: Tailor to your specialty and location
- General liability: Covers non-clinical claims (e.g., slip and falls)
- Employment practices liability (EPLI): Covers wrongful termination, harassment, discrimination
- Umbrella policy: Provides extra coverage above other limits

Pros:

- High protection for relatively low cost

Cons:

- Won't cover everything

- Must understand exclusions and gaps

Action Step: Get an insurance audit. Make sure your coverage limits match your net worth and risk level.

1. **Use Retirement Accounts Wisely** Most retirement accounts are protected from creditors by law.

- 401(k), SEP IRA, Defined Benefit Plans: Federal protections
- IRAs: Protected in many states (check your local laws)

Pros:

- Asset growth + protection = double benefit

Cons:

- Cannot access early without penalties (usually)

Action Step: Max out contributions annually, especially to plans that offer legal protection.

1. **Homestead Exemption** Some states protect your primary residence up to a certain value.

- Florida and Texas: Strong protection
- Other states: Varies widely

Action Step: Learn your state's homestead laws. Consider whether using a trust or changing title offers better protection.

1. **Titling Assets Correctly**

- Joint Tenancy with Right of Survivorship (JTWROS)
- Tenants by the Entirety (for married couples, in some states)
- Separate ownership to avoid joint liability

Action Step: Review how all major assets are titled. Fix mismatches between your estate plan and legal ownership.

1. **Asset Protection Trusts** These trusts are designed to move assets out of your personal name while still allowing you to benefit from them.

- Domestic Asset Protection Trusts (DAPTs): Available in certain states
- Offshore trusts: More complex, higher cost, but powerful in some scenarios

Pros:

- High level of protection

Cons:

- Expensive to set up and maintain
- Must be done well in advance of any legal claim

Action Step: Talk to your estate attorney if your net worth exceeds $3M or your risk profile is unusually high.

1. **Avoid Personal Guarantees Where Possible**

- Lenders may ask you to personally guarantee business loans, leases, or lines of credit

Action Step: Negotiate to limit or remove personal guarantees as your business matures. Consider liability if something goes wrong.

Mistakes Dentists Make with Asset Protection

1. **Thinking malpractice insurance is enough**
2. **Putting everything in joint accounts**
3. **Ignoring entity formalities (commingling funds, missing filings)**
4. **Waiting too long to act**
5. **Failing to update asset protection as net worth grows**

Action Step: Choose one mistake above that might apply to you. Fix it this month.

How to Build an Asset Protection Team

Asset protection isn't DIY. Your team should include:

- Business attorney
- Estate planning attorney
- Financial advisor
- CPA (especially for entity structure and retirement planning)
- Insurance broker

Action Step: Set a goal to meet with your full financial team once a year. Coordinate your asset protection strategy across all professionals.

Integrating Asset Protection with Financial Planning

Your asset protection plan should align with:

- Your estate plan
- Your retirement timeline
- Your debt strategy
- Your business exit or transition plan

For example:

- Trusts used in estate planning may also protect assets
- Business structures used for tax efficiency may also limit liability

Action Step: Ask your financial advisor to map your entire financial picture—including how each part is protected.

Real-World Scenario: The "What If" Exercise

Imagine:

- You're sued for an accident outside your practice
- A patient files a high-profile complaint
- An employee claims discrimination
- Your business partner files for bankruptcy

What would happen to:

- Your home?
- Your retirement accounts?
- Your practice bank account?
- Your child's college fund?

Action Step: Walk through this exercise with your advisor. Don't just hope—prepare.

Closing Thoughts: It's Not About Fear. It's About Freedom.

Protecting your assets isn't about living in fear. It's about sleeping better at night.

It's about knowing that no matter what happens—lawsuit, downturn, partnership dispute, or personal curveball—your wealth, your family, and your future are protected.

So don't wait. Don't wing it. Don't assume insurance is enough.

Build your walls. Tighten your defenses. Own your peace of mind.

You've worked too hard to leave it all exposed.

You've got this. Let's protect it—together.

Chapter 21: Dual-Income Households – Coordinating Finances

Let's be honest—love and money don't always mix easily.

And when both partners are earning significant incomes—especially in demanding, high-stress professions like dentistry—the financial dynamic becomes even more complex. There's more opportunity, yes. But also more decisions to make, more calendars to juggle, more goals to align, and more pressure to "get it right."

This chapter is about helping you do just that.

Whether you and your spouse are both dentists, one of you is a healthcare provider and the other is in a different field, or you're navigating entrepreneurship together, this chapter is your guide to coordinating finances as a dual-income household.

It's about clarity, connection, and the kind of financial teamwork that supports—not strains—your relationship.

Let's talk about what it takes to build a united front around money, while still honoring who each of you are as individuals.

Why Dual-Income Households Need a Plan

Two incomes should make things easier, right?

In theory, yes. But in practice, it can lead to:

- Confusion about who pays for what
- Differences in saving or spending habits
- Mismatched financial goals

- Power dynamics tied to income levels
- "Yours vs. mine" mentalities

The key is intention.

When both partners are financially capable, the real challenge isn't survival—it's synergy.

Action Step: Ask yourself: Are we building our financial life *together*—or just living side-by-side?

Start With the Big Conversations

Before you talk numbers, talk values.

Sit down and ask each other:

- What did money look like in your house growing up?
- What's your earliest memory about money?
- What financial fears do you carry?
- What does financial freedom mean to you?
- How do you want to handle finances as a team?

These aren't just "get to know you" questions. They're the foundation for every joint decision you'll make.

Action Step: Set aside a "money talk" date night. Ask each other the questions above. Listen more than you speak.

Choosing a Financial Structure That Works

There's no one right way to manage dual-income finances. Options include:

1. **Fully Combined:** All income goes into joint accounts; shared budgeting and spending
2. **Partially Combined:** Joint account for bills and goals; separate accounts for personal spending
3. **Completely Separate:** Each person manages their own money and contributes proportionally to joint expenses

Pros and Cons:

Fully Combined Pros:

- Full transparency
- Easier to align on shared goals
- Often feels more "unified"

Cons:

- Can feel like loss of autonomy
- May spark resentment if spending habits differ

Partially Combined Pros:

- Allows autonomy and shared responsibility
- Works well with unequal incomes

Cons:

- Requires clear communication and systems
- Can still create misunderstandings if not maintained

Completely Separate Pros:

- Full autonomy
- Easy to track individual spending

Cons:

- Can feel like roommates
- Harder to plan long-term goals as a team

Action Step: Choose a structure that reflects your personalities, income levels, and communication style. Revisit it annually.

Aligning Goals, Timelines, and Trade-Offs

Even high earners need to prioritize.

Sit down and list your top financial goals:

- Paying off debt
- Buying a home
- Starting a practice
- Saving for kids' education
- Funding retirement
- Travel or big life experiences

Then:

- Rank them in order of importance (individually, then together)
- Estimate the timelines for each
- Talk through trade-offs

You may find:

- One of you is focused on paying down debt
- The other wants to aggressively invest
- One is more risk-tolerant than the other

This is where real planning starts—not with spreadsheets, but with shared vision.

Action Step: Create a joint financial "vision board." You can use paper, Pinterest, or a whiteboard. Make it visual.

Handling Income Inequality with Respect and Clarity

One of you may earn more—and that's okay.

The challenge is to:

- Avoid resentment

- Recognize non-financial contributions (childcare, housework, emotional labor)
- Share decision-making power, even if income isn't equal

If you're the higher earner:

- Be mindful not to dominate decisions
- Don't weaponize your income

If you're the lower earner:

- Speak up—your voice matters
- Don't defer just because you bring home less

Action Step: Consider splitting shared expenses by percentage of income, not 50/50. This balances equity with fairness.

Building a Joint Budget That Actually Works

The key to joint budgeting isn't just numbers—it's clarity and buy-in.

Steps:

1. Track all household income
2. List fixed expenses (mortgage, utilities, loans)
3. Estimate variable expenses (groceries, gas, gifts)
4. Include financial goals (savings, investments)
5. Allocate "fun money" for each partner
6. Review monthly and adjust as needed

Tools to consider:

- YNAB (You Need a Budget)
- Mint
- Monarch Money
- Google Sheets or Excel

Action Step: Schedule a monthly "money huddle." Keep it short, respectful, and goal-focused. Make it a habit.

Tax Planning as a Dual-Income Household

Dual incomes can mean:

- Higher marginal tax rates
- AMT (Alternative Minimum Tax) exposure
- Loss of deductions or credits
- Opportunity for smart strategies

Work with a CPA who can help you:

- Optimize withholdings
- Use retirement contributions to lower taxable income
- Evaluate filing jointly vs. separately
- Maximize deductions for practice expenses or home offices

Action Step: Schedule a pre-year-end tax review with your CPA. Don't leave thousands on the table.

Insurance and Protection Planning

Two incomes = two lives that need protection.

Review:

- Life insurance: Enough to replace income or support children?
- Disability insurance: Especially important for dentists
- Health insurance: Joint plan vs. separate employer plans
- Long-term care: Plan early if one partner is a caregiver

Action Step: Create a protection plan. What if one of you couldn't work for 12 months? How would you adjust?

Investment Strategy for Couples

You need one portfolio—not two that work in opposite directions.

Coordinate:

- Risk tolerance
- Asset allocation
- Tax-efficient account placement (Roth, IRA, 401(k), brokerage)
- Practice equity vs. market equity

Work with an advisor who:

- Plans for both of you
- Reviews accounts together
- Keeps you focused on long-term goals

Action Step: Consolidate where it makes sense. Schedule an annual review of *both* your investment accounts.

Estate Planning and Legal Documents

If you're building wealth together, protect it together.

You need:

- Wills
- Powers of attorney (financial + healthcare)
- Healthcare directives
- Beneficiary designations
- Trusts (if appropriate)

Don't assume everything "just goes" to your spouse automatically.

Action Step: Meet with an estate planning attorney. Create or update your documents with both partners present.

Conflict, Communication, and Financial Teamwork

Disagreements are normal. Avoid these traps:

- Avoiding money conversations
- Assigning blame
- Hiding purchases or accounts
- Letting resentment build

Better habits:

- Use "I" statements
- Set regular check-in times
- Have shared and individual spending limits
- Agree on a problem-solving process

Real-World Tip: Keep a shared financial journal. When something comes up, write it down first. Then discuss when you're both calm.

Closing Thoughts: Two Incomes, One Vision

Money shouldn't pull you apart—it should bring you together.

Coordinating finances as a dual-income couple isn't about merging everything or thinking exactly alike. It's about:

- Listening
- Planning
- Adjusting
- Growing

You don't have to be perfect. You just have to be present.

So talk often. Plan together. Dream out loud.

Because two incomes mean two minds, two hearts, and one powerful opportunity to build something meaningful together.

Chapter 22: Buying Into or Starting a Practice

Let's start with one truth every dentist knows in their gut:

There's a difference between working *in* a practice and owning one.

For many dentists, ownership is the dream. It's about autonomy. Leadership. Building equity. Practicing your way, on your terms. It's also about risk—and reward. Because while owning a dental practice can be one of the most powerful financial and personal decisions of your career, it's also one of the most complex.

This chapter is here to walk you through that decision: whether to buy into an existing practice or build your own from scratch.

We'll unpack the financial details, the emotional roadblocks, the real-world logistics, and the questions you didn't know to ask—so you can make your move with confidence and clarity.

Whether you're a few years out of school or deep into your associate career and itching for ownership, this is your guide.

Let's dig in.

Why Ownership Matters

There's nothing wrong with being an associate. For many dentists, it's the right fit.

But if you've ever said:

- "I wish I had more control."

- "I feel like I'm building someone else's dream."
- "I want to build long-term wealth."
- "I want to shape the culture of my own team."

...then ownership is worth exploring.

Owning a practice can provide:

- Income growth
- Tax advantages
- Equity building
- Creative control
- Leadership and legacy opportunities

Action Step: Ask yourself: What's driving your interest in ownership—freedom, income, leadership, or something else? Get clear.

Ownership Path #1: Buying Into a Practice

This means purchasing a share of an existing practice, often with the goal of becoming a full partner or sole owner over time.

Pros:

- Immediate patient base
- Existing staff and systems
- Lower startup risk
- Mentorship from existing owner(s)

Cons:

- Less control initially
- Potential conflict with partner(s)
- Need to align values and vision

When it works well, a buy-in can be a springboard into stable, supported ownership. When it doesn't, it's a messy divorce.

Action Step: Before any buy-in discussion, ask for:

- Full financials (P&L, balance sheets, production reports)
- Historical practice performance
- Current debt obligations
- Patient demographics and flow
- Breakdown of staff compensation and turnover

Ownership Path #2: Starting a Practice From Scratch

Building your own practice from the ground up is bold—and for the right person, incredibly rewarding.

Pros:

- Full control over brand, systems, and culture
- Can build to match your vision
- No legacy issues or partner conflicts

Cons:

- High upfront cost
- No immediate revenue
- Longer path to profitability
- Requires strong leadership and grit

Real-World Story: Dr. R opened a startup practice with $500k in loans. She broke even at 14 months, grew to $1.2M revenue by year three, and opened a second location by year five. The key? Strong community marketing, a lean team, and operational discipline.

Action Step: Interview at least two practice owners who started from scratch. Ask what they wish they had known.

Choosing the Right Path for You

Ask yourself:

- Do I want control or stability?
- Am I entrepreneurial or do I prefer structure?
- Do I thrive in building something from nothing—or improving something that exists?
- What's my financial risk tolerance?

Then weigh your:

- Personal life stage (family, debt, flexibility)
- Location preferences
- Available capital and financing options
- Network and mentorship support

Action Step: Make a decision matrix. List your priorities, rate each path against them, and see where the numbers point you.

Financing Your Ownership Dream

Buying or starting a practice is a big financial leap—but it's also an investment.

Sources of funding:

- Bank loans (specialty lenders for dental practices)
- SBA loans
- Seller financing (for buy-ins or buy-outs)
- Personal savings or family support

You'll need:

- A solid business plan
- Personal financial statement
- Good credit history
- Cash flow projections

Action Step: Talk to a dental-specific lender early. They can help you understand your borrowing power and what you'll need to prepare.

What to Look for in a Buy-In or Acquisition

When evaluating a practice to buy or join, consider:

- Location and real estate (ownership vs. lease)
- Practice valuation method (asset-based, income-based, market comps)
- Patient base size and demographics
- Staff structure and morale
- Equipment and technology age
- Community reputation
- Insurance mix (fee-for-service vs. PPO vs. Medicaid)

Action Step: Hire a dental CPA or consultant to review the numbers. Don't go it alone.

Building a Startup: What to Expect

Timeline:

- 6–12 months to plan, secure financing, and build out
- 6–18 months to break even
- 2–5 years to reach full profitability

Key steps:

- Create a detailed business plan
- Choose location and negotiate lease or real estate purchase
- Design and build the office
- Hire staff (often part-time to start)
- Market aggressively (community, social media, local businesses)

Pro Tip: Start lean. You don't need every bell and whistle on day one.

Action Step: Map out a 24-month projection of expenses, revenue, and breakeven point. Know your numbers.

The Legal Side of Ownership

Work with a business attorney to:

- Structure your entity (LLC, S-Corp)
- Draft or review partnership agreements
- Review or negotiate leases
- Handle employment agreements and handbooks

Action Step: Schedule a consultation before signing *anything*. Legal fees upfront are cheaper than litigation later.

Tax Considerations of Ownership

Owning a practice changes your tax situation dramatically:

- You can deduct legitimate business expenses
- You must manage payroll taxes if you have employees
- You can create retirement plans (Solo 401(k), SEP IRA, Defined Benefit Plan)
- You'll need quarterly estimated taxes

Action Step: Work with a CPA who understands dental practices. They should help you minimize tax liability *and* maximize strategy.

Insurance You'll Need as an Owner

Protect your investment with:

- Malpractice insurance
- Business owner's policy (BOP)
- General liability
- Workers' comp
- Disability (especially for yourself)
- Cybersecurity and data breach coverage

Action Step: Get an insurance audit. Make sure every angle is covered.

Staffing and Culture: Your Greatest Asset

Your team will make or break your practice.

From day one:

- Hire slowly and intentionally
- Build a culture of trust, accountability, and patient care
- Train on systems, communication, and service
- Lead with clarity and consistency

Action Step: Create a vision statement and core values for your practice. Use them in every hiring decision.

Closing Thoughts: Ownership Is the Starting Line, Not the Finish Line

Owning a practice isn't a destination. It's a platform.

It's the place from which you build wealth, leadership, freedom, and legacy. It's where your financial plan, career growth, and personal vision converge.

It's not easy—but it's worth it.

So if your gut is saying it's time—listen. If you're not sure, ask the questions. Do the homework. Talk to those who've walked the path.

Because with the right plan, the right mindset, and the right support—you can build something not just profitable, but powerful.

You've got this. And your practice—the one with your name on the door—might just be the next step.

Chapter 23: Real Estate Decisions – Practice vs. Personal

Let's talk about one of the most emotional and financially significant topics in any dentist's life: real estate.

Real estate touches everything—from where you live and raise your family to where you practice and build your career. It's deeply personal, but also deeply strategic. And the decisions you make—about buying vs. renting, investing or holding, leasing or owning—can shape your financial life in ways that ripple for decades.

This chapter is your guide to understanding how real estate plays into both sides of your financial picture: your practice and your personal life. It's about making choices that align with your goals, not just what "everyone else" seems to be doing.

We'll walk through the big questions, the pros and cons, the numbers, the emotions, and the strategic opportunities—all through the lens of what matters most: building a life and a career you're proud of.

Let's dive in.

Why Real Estate Matters to Dentists

Real estate is one of the biggest financial decisions you'll ever make.

But here's the problem: a lot of dentists treat it like a checkbox. Buy a home. Lease a space. Done.

But when you pause and ask the right questions, real estate can become:

- A way to build long-term wealth

- A tax strategy
- A lifestyle design tool
- A business growth platform
- A retirement plan

That's what this chapter is about.

Action Step: Think about your current real estate situation. Do your home and practice locations reflect where you want your life and career to go?

Part I: Practice Real Estate – Lease or Buy?

This is the first major decision for most practice owners: should you lease your space or buy your building?

Let's break it down.

Leasing Your Practice Space

Pros:

- Lower upfront costs
- More flexibility
- Often faster to get started
- Maintenance and repairs often covered by landlord

Cons:

- No equity or asset growth
- Subject to rent increases
- Limited control over space
- Risk of being forced to move

Buying Your Practice Building

Pros:

- Build equity over time
- Stable costs (especially with fixed-rate mortgage)

- Can customize the space
- May provide rental income if you sublease

Cons:

- High upfront costs
- Less flexibility to move or expand
- Responsibility for maintenance, taxes, insurance

Real-World Example: Dr. C leased a space in a high-traffic retail center. Her rent increased 30% over five years. She eventually bought a small building nearby, renovated it, and locked in a fixed mortgage—saving over $2,000 per month long-term.

Action Step: Run a 10-year cost comparison for your current lease vs. a purchase option in your area. Include down payment, loan terms, maintenance, taxes, and appreciation.

How to Evaluate a Practice Building Purchase

If you're considering buying, here's what to evaluate:

- Location (visibility, parking, accessibility)
- Zoning and compliance with dental use
- Condition of the building (HVAC, roof, plumbing)
- Potential for expansion
- Resale or lease value if you move

Financing Options:

- Conventional loan
- SBA 7(a) or 504 loan (favorable terms for healthcare)
- Commercial real estate lender with dental experience

Tax Tip: If structured properly, your practice can lease the building from an entity you own—creating rent deductions for the business and income for you.

Action Step: Talk to a dental-specific lender and CPA before you make an offer. They'll help you structure it smartly.

Owning Practice Real Estate as an Investment

Buying your own building isn't just a business decision—it can be an investment strategy.

Many dentists:

- Own the building through an LLC
- Lease to their practice (passive income)
- Hold the property after retiring (sell the practice, keep the building)
- Use 1031 exchanges to defer capital gains on sale

Pros:

- Long-term wealth builder
- Retirement income stream

Cons:

- Illiquid
- Management responsibilities

Action Step: Ask your financial planner to model your long-term net worth with and without real estate ownership. Run the numbers.

Part II: Personal Real Estate – Should Dentists Buy a Home?

The classic American dream: homeownership.

But for many dentists, especially early in their careers, it's not always the smartest first move.

Pros of Buying a Home:

- Build equity over time
- Stable housing costs (with fixed mortgage)

- Potential tax deductions (interest, property tax)
- Freedom to renovate and customize

Cons:

- High upfront costs (down payment, closing)
- Ongoing maintenance expenses
- Tied to a location (less flexibility)
- Risk of market downturns

Key Considerations:

- Student loan payments
- Job stability or location changes
- Practice start-up or ownership plans

Real-World Story: Dr. T bought a house right out of school, then took an associate job in another city. She had to rent it out at a loss for three years.

Action Step: Ask: Am I financially stable enough to buy—and emotionally ready to stay put for at least 5–7 years?

Renting Isn't Throwing Money Away

This is worth repeating.

Renting can be a strategic choice if:

- You're early in your career
- You're relocating often
- You're saving for a big practice down payment
- You want to stay nimble

Action Step: Calculate your "rent vs. buy" break-even point using an online calculator. Consider appreciation, taxes, and closing costs.

How to Choose Between Buying a Home and Buying a Practice First

Many dentists can't do both at once.

In most cases:

- Prioritize buying a practice (higher ROI, income growth)
- Rent your home if needed

Why?

- Practices often appreciate faster than homes
- Practice ownership increases income
- Home buying gets easier with better cash flow and credit profile

Action Step: Create a 3–5 year plan. What comes first—and how will it position you for the next step?

Real Estate as a Wealth-Building Strategy (Beyond Your Practice)

Once your career and finances stabilize, real estate can become a powerful secondary wealth-building vehicle.

Options:

- Residential rental properties
- Commercial buildings
- REITs (real estate investment trusts)
- Short-term rentals (Airbnb, etc.)

Pros:

- Diversification
- Cash flow
- Appreciation

Cons:

- Management headaches
- Market risk

- Illiquidity

Action Step: Consider investing in one rental property—or partnering with a property manager—to explore real estate without overextending.

Work With the Right Real Estate Team

As a dentist, you need a team that understands your goals:

- Commercial broker (for practice space)
- Residential agent (for home)
- Dental lender
- Real estate attorney (especially for commercial deals)
- CPA and financial advisor (for tax and investment implications)

Action Step: Interview at least three real estate professionals before choosing. Ask about experience with dentists specifically.

Closing Thoughts: Your Real Estate Strategy Is Part of Your Life Strategy

Don't buy because you "should." Don't lease because it's easier. Don't rush into a home because your classmates did.

Make real estate decisions based on:

- Your vision
- Your numbers
- Your lifestyle
- Your business plan

You can use real estate to build wealth, reduce stress, and align your environment with your goals.

But only if you pause, plan, and personalize it.

So take the time. Run the numbers. Ask the questions.

And remember: This isn't just about buildings. It's about building a life.

You've got this.

Chapter 24: Charitable Giving, Gifting, and Legacy Planning

Let's step back for a moment.

You've worked hard. You've built a practice, served your community, paid down debt, made smart investments, and maybe even created wealth. But as your career evolves—and your perspective shifts—you might find yourself asking bigger questions:

"What's all this for?" "What do I want to leave behind?" "How can I use what I've earned to help others—and build something that lasts?"

This chapter is about those questions.

It's about charitable giving, legacy planning, and the kind of financial choices that go beyond just spreadsheets and balances. It's about meaning.

Whether you're a new dentist thinking ahead or a mid-career owner wondering how to give back, this chapter is your compass for creating impact—with clarity, intention, and smart planning.

Why Charitable Giving Matters (Financially and Emotionally)

Charitable giving isn't just about donations—it's about direction.

It lets you:

- Support causes and communities you care about
- Teach values to your children or team
- Create a deeper purpose behind your work
- Reduce your taxable income
- Inspire your staff, patients, and peers

And when it's done right, it doesn't take away from your financial goals—it strengthens them.

Action Step: Take a moment and write down three causes or communities that have shaped your life. These are often your giving "north stars."

Giving Isn't One-Size-Fits-All

There are many ways to give—some formal, some simple, some deeply strategic.

Types of Giving:

- One-time donations
- Recurring monthly gifts
- Donor-advised funds (DAFs)
- Charitable trusts
- Legacy gifts through your will or estate
- Volunteering your time or services

Each has a different financial and emotional return.

Real-World Example: Dr. J tithes 10% of her practice revenue each month to support free dental care clinics and scholarships for first-gen dental students. It's automatic, tax-deductible, and deeply personal.

Action Step: Choose one giving method that fits your style and your season of life. You can always expand later.

The Tax Benefits of Giving

The IRS encourages generosity—but the rules can be tricky.

Standard Deduction vs. Itemizing:

- If you don't itemize, you may not see tax savings from charitable gifts
- But with proper planning, large donations or giving strategies can create meaningful deductions

Qualified Charitable Distributions (QCDs):

- For those over 70½, you can donate up to $100,000/year from an IRA directly to charity—tax-free

Donating Appreciated Assets:

- Stocks or real estate held more than a year can be donated to avoid capital gains taxes *and* get a deduction

Action Step: Work with a CPA or financial planner to align your giving with tax strategy. Especially in high-income years.

Donor-Advised Funds (DAFs): A Powerful Giving Tool

Think of a DAF as a "charitable investment account."

You contribute money, take the deduction now, and grant the funds to your favorite charities over time.

Pros:

- Immediate tax deduction
- You can invest the funds to grow over time
- Great for years with big income (e.g., practice sale)

Cons:

- Irrevocable (you can't take it back)
- Requires setup and tracking

Real-World Story: Dr. S sold her practice and contributed $100,000 to a DAF that year—lowering her taxable income and creating a fund she now grants from each Christmas with her kids.

Action Step: If you have a high-income year coming, open a DAF and pre-fund your giving goals.

Creating a Charitable Giving Plan

1. Identify your causes (faith, education, healthcare, local)
2. Set an annual giving budget (e.g., 5–10% of net income)

3. Choose your methods (cash, DAF, appreciated assets)
4. Involve your family or team (to teach and inspire)
5. Track your giving like you track other goals

Action Step: Add a "giving line item" to your annual financial plan. Make it part of your strategy, not an afterthought.

Gifting to Family: Generosity Without Guilt or Chaos

Gifting to your kids, grandkids, or other family members is its own kind of giving.

Annual Gift Tax Exclusion (2024):

- You can give up to $17,000 per person, per year, tax-free
- Married couples can double this to $34,000

Lifetime Gift and Estate Exemption:

- You can give millions over your lifetime without tax—but large gifts may require IRS reporting

Smart Ways to Gift:

- Fund a 529 plan for education
- Help with down payments (documented clearly)
- Gift appreciated assets instead of cash (for tax benefits)

Real-World Story: Dr. M gifted $10,000 each to his three children in Roth IRA contributions by hiring them part-time in the office and using their earned income as the basis.

Action Step: Consider how your financial plan can help family—not just leave them money, but teach them financial literacy and responsibility.

Legacy Planning: Building Something That Outlives You

Legacy planning means creating a financial impact beyond your lifetime. It's about:

- Estate planning (wills, trusts, beneficiary designations)
- Passing on values, not just valuables
- Structuring charitable gifts after death
- Preparing heirs with financial education

Questions to Ask:

- What do I want to be remembered for?
- What do I want my kids or team to carry forward?
- What problems in the world do I want to help solve?

Action Step: Write a one-page legacy letter. Not a legal document—just your story, values, and wishes for your family and community.

Setting Up a Charitable Trust

For high-net-worth dentists, a charitable trust can:

- Provide income now
- Offer tax deductions
- Leave assets to a cause you care about

Types:

- Charitable Remainder Trust (CRT)
- Charitable Lead Trust (CLT)

Complex but powerful. Work with an estate attorney.

Action Step: If your net worth exceeds $5M or you're planning a major liquidity event, ask your attorney about trust-based giving strategies.

Using Your Practice as a Platform for Giving

You can give through your business:

- Pro bono dental days
- Patient care scholarships

- Partnerships with nonprofits
- Rounding up or matching patient donations
- Giving a portion of profits to a cause

This builds:

- Community goodwill
- Patient loyalty
- Team morale

Real-World Example: Dr. B hosts an annual "Smiles for Service" day, offering free care to veterans. Her staff rallies around it—and her community does too.

Action Step: Choose one charitable initiative to embed into your practice culture this year.

Teaching Giving to the Next Generation

Legacy isn't just what you leave—it's what you *teach*.

Involve your kids or grandkids:

- Let them choose causes for family gifts
- Give them a DAF with a small budget to manage
- Match their charitable efforts
- Share the "why" behind your giving

Action Step: Start a family giving tradition. Make it part of birthdays, holidays, or annual reviews.

Closing Thoughts: Wealth Is What You Build. Legacy Is What You Give.

Your career is more than income. Your financial plan is more than spreadsheets. Your wealth is more than your net worth.

You have the power to:

- Heal people with your hands
- Support people with your earnings

- Shape the future with your values

So whether it's a small monthly gift, a planned trust, a scholarship fund, or a note to your children—start your giving now.

You don't have to be ultra-wealthy. You just have to be willing.

Because when your money serves your mission—it multiplies.

You've got this. Let's give well.

Part 3: Protecting and Growing Your Wealth

Part 3 of *Financial Literacy For Dentists* marks a turning point in your financial journey—from making money to making it work for you. After years of education and early career building, the focus now shifts to two essential goals: protecting what you've built and growing it wisely. This section is about turning income into impact, earnings into security, and opportunity into lasting wealth.

We begin with the foundation of financial protection. As income increases and responsibilities grow—whether it's a mortgage, a family, a practice, or all of the above—so does the need for comprehensive risk management. We walk through the critical insurances every dentist should understand and likely have: malpractice, disability, life, business overhead, and umbrella liability coverage. This isn't just about worst-case scenarios—it's about safeguarding your lifestyle and legacy.

From there, we pivot to wealth building. You'll learn how to:

- Build a diversified investment portfolio tailored to your risk tolerance and time horizon
- Choose between retirement plans like 401(k)s, Roth IRAs, SEP IRAs, and defined benefit plans
- Understand tax-advantaged investing and how to keep more of what you earn
- Make smart real estate decisions—whether you're buying a home,

investing in rental property, or purchasing a practice building

But this part isn't just about numbers—it's also about behavior. We cover how to avoid lifestyle inflation, manage the pressure to "look successful," and make intentional financial decisions that align with your values. This section equips you with the strategies to protect your time, peace of mind, and financial future—while still enjoying the rewards of your hard work.

By the end of Part 3, you'll have:

- A clear understanding of how to protect your assets and your earning power
- A plan for growing long-term wealth through investing and tax-smart strategies
- A framework to balance enjoying life today with planning for tomorrow

This section is your playbook for building wealth that doesn't just look good on paper—but actually works for your real life.

Chapter 25: Caring for Your Family Through Financial Planning

Let's talk about what really matters.

Because when all the spreadsheets are closed, the practice is locked up, and the noise of the day quiets down, what most dentists are truly working for—what they carry in their hearts—is their family.

Financial planning isn't just about growing wealth or minimizing taxes. It's about taking care of the people you love. Protecting them. Supporting their dreams. Giving them security, opportunities, and peace of mind—even when you're not there to do it yourself.

This chapter is about that kind of planning.

It's about how dentists—whether new in their careers or decades into ownership—can use money not just as a tool for progress, but as an instrument of care.

Whether you're raising young kids, supporting aging parents, or planning a legacy for the next generation, this chapter will help you create a plan that holds your family's future in steady, capable hands.

Why Family Should Be at the Center of Your Plan

You became a dentist for many reasons. But if you have a partner, children, parents, or people who depend on you, they've likely become the reason you keep going.

So let's move financial planning beyond numbers and put it where it belongs: in service of the people you care about.

Planning for your family means:

- Protecting income if something happens to you
- Ensuring your kids can go to college without debt
- Helping your spouse feel safe and supported
- Preparing your estate to transfer wealth without confusion
- Modeling financial wisdom for the next generation

Action Step: Ask yourself: If something happened to me tomorrow, would my family know what to do? Would they be okay?

Start With the Essentials: Income Protection

Life Insurance

If you have dependents, life insurance is non-negotiable. It replaces your income, pays off debt, and buys your family time to grieve without financial panic.

Types:

- Term: Low-cost, simple, good for income replacement
- Whole or Permanent: Higher cost, includes cash value, useful in some advanced planning scenarios

How much? A general rule is 10–15x your annual income, but a detailed needs analysis is better.

Disability Insurance

If you can't work, you can't earn. And dentistry is a hands-on profession—disability can end your career.

Key factors:

- Own-occupation coverage is a must
- Don't rely solely on employer plans—they may not cover enough

Action Step: Get a full insurance audit. Make sure your family would have enough coverage to replace your income and cover major expenses.

Building a Family-Centered Financial Plan

Step 1: Define Your Family Goals

- College savings?
- Helping parents financially?
- Taking a sabbatical to spend more time at home?
- Leaving an inheritance?

Step 2: Create Separate Buckets for Each Goal

- Emergency fund
- Education savings (529, UTMA, brokerage)
- Retirement (401(k), IRA, practice sale)
- General investing (for mid-term goals)

Step 3: Automate and Adjust

- Set up automatic contributions
- Review quarterly or semi-annually
- Update as life changes (new baby, job change, etc.)

Action Step: Write out your top three family-focused financial goals. Then tie one financial account or tool to each.

Planning for Children: Now and in the Future

Education Savings

529 plans are a tax-advantaged way to save for college:

- Grows tax-free
- Withdrawals for qualified expenses are tax-free
- Some states offer tax deductions for contributions

Other Options:

- UTMA accounts (less tax-efficient, but more flexible)
- Roth IRA (for teens with earned income)

Teaching Kids About Money

Your example is their curriculum.

Tips:

- Talk openly about money (age-appropriate)
- Use allowance as a teaching tool
- Involve them in charitable giving
- Let them make low-stakes financial mistakes

Action Step: Open a 529 plan for each child. Set a recurring monthly contribution, even if it's small.

Planning With a Spouse or Partner

If you share finances, you need shared vision.

Key conversations:

- Are we aligned on spending vs. saving?
- What are our shared goals for our children?
- What happens financially if one of us passes away?
- Do we want to retire at the same time?

Shared Tools:

- Monthly or quarterly money check-ins
- Joint financial dashboard (e.g., Monarch, Tiller)
- Estate plan that protects both partners

Action Step: Schedule a monthly "financial date." Keep it low-pressure. Use it to reflect, plan, and realign.

Supporting Aging Parents or Extended Family

For many dentists, this becomes a chapter of life:

- Helping pay for a parent's medical care
- Managing finances for someone with declining capacity

- Balancing your own retirement with caregiving costs

Planning Ahead Helps:

- Talk early and often about expectations
- Understand your parents' insurance, assets, and wishes
- Build long-term care planning into your own financial plan

Action Step: Have a family conversation. Ask your parents about their wishes, documents, and what support they may need down the road.

Estate Planning: Because They Deserve Clarity

Estate planning is a gift to your family.

It prevents confusion, avoids conflict, and ensures that your assets go where they should.

Must-Have Documents:

- Will
- Trust (revocable or irrevocable, depending on goals)
- Durable power of attorney
- Healthcare directive
- Guardianship designation (if you have minor children)

Beneficiary Designations:

- IRAs, 401(k)s, life insurance—make sure these are up to date

Letter of Intent:

- Optional, but powerful: Write a personal note or guide for your family explaining your wishes and values

Action Step: Schedule a meeting with an estate planning attorney. Start with the basics. Don't wait.

What Happens to the Practice?

If you own a dental practice:

- Who will take over if you pass away?
- Is there a buy-sell agreement in place?
- Will your family get fair compensation for your equity?

Solutions:

- Key person insurance
- Practice succession planning
- Emergency transition plan (short-term and long-term)

Action Step: Review your practice continuity plan. Ask: Can my family access the value I've built here if I'm gone?

Teaching Financial Literacy to Your Family

Passing on wealth is one thing. Passing on wisdom is another.

How to teach:

- Share your financial values at the dinner table
- Let kids "earn and learn" through small jobs
- Involve teens in budgeting and investing
- Use milestones (16th birthday, college) to expand financial responsibility

Real-World Tip: Create a family financial binder or shared Google Drive folder. Include key contacts, policies, accounts, and instructions.

Action Step: Host a yearly "family finance day." Make it a tradition. Share what matters and what's next.

Closing Thoughts: Your Legacy Starts With Today

Taking care of your family through financial planning isn't about big grand gestures. It's about the quiet, steady steps you take every day:

- Saving consistently
- Protecting what matters
- Planning ahead
- Communicating openly

You don't have to be perfect. You just have to be intentional.

Because what your family will remember isn't just how much money you had—it's the peace, security, and values you gave them.

So take the next step. Build the plan. Make it personal.

You've got this. And your family's future will be stronger because of it.

Chapter 26: Burnout and Its Financial Consequences

Let's start with something most dentists don't say out loud:

"I'm exhausted."

Not just physically. But emotionally. Mentally. Sometimes spiritually.

You're not alone.

Burnout is real in dentistry—and it's more than just a buzzword. It's a chronic state of stress and disconnection that can quietly erode not just your well-being, but your finances, relationships, and future.

This chapter is about naming it, understanding it, and building a plan to protect both your peace *and* your portfolio.

Because burnout doesn't just cost you emotionally—it can cost you thousands (or even millions) if it goes unaddressed.

Whether you're deep in the fog or just starting to feel the edge, this chapter is your safe place to pause, reflect, and take real steps forward.

What Is Burnout (and Why It Hits Dentists So Hard)?

Burnout is more than being tired. It's:

- Emotional exhaustion
- Detachment from work and patients
- A reduced sense of personal accomplishment

Dentists are especially vulnerable because:

- You manage physical labor + emotional labor
- You run a business *and* provide clinical care
- You often work in isolation
- Patient anxiety becomes your daily emotional backdrop

Real Talk: Burnout doesn't mean you're weak. It means you're human—and likely operating at an unsustainable pace.

The Financial Costs of Burnout

Burnout doesn't just show up in your mood. It shows up on your balance sheet.

How burnout costs you money:

- Reduced productivity or fewer clinical hours
- Early retirement due to exhaustion
- Hiring costly associates to reduce load
- More sick days and unplanned absences
- Lower case acceptance from emotional disengagement
- Increased staff turnover from toxic stress culture
- Mistakes that lead to malpractice risk

Long-Term Impact:

- Lower lifetime earnings
- Depleted retirement savings from career exits or scaling back
- Increased therapy and health expenses
- Missed opportunities (real estate, business growth, etc.)

Action Step: Look at your last 12 months. Did burnout lead to any direct financial loss? Time off, lost revenue, higher team churn?

Signs Burnout May Be Hurting Your Financial Future

- You dread going to work—even after a weekend
- You've stopped doing treatment you once enjoyed

- Your collections are dropping, but your hours aren't
- You find yourself saying, "I just need to get through this month" over and over
- You're spending more on coping (retail therapy, unhealthy habits)

Action Step: Write down the top three ways burnout has affected your money. No shame—just awareness.

Burnout and the "Golden Handcuffs" Trap

Many dentists stay in stressful roles because they feel they can't afford to stop:

- Huge monthly expenses
- Private school tuition
- Practice loans
- Lifestyle expectations

But staying in burnout for money's sake usually backfires.

You may hold onto income—but lose your health, your marriage, or your love for the profession.

Action Step: Ask: What financial obligations are keeping me stuck—and are they really non-negotiable?

The Cost of Ignoring It vs. The Cost of Addressing It

Ignoring burnout:

- Constant tension
- Worsening performance
- Disconnection from patients and team
- Reactive decision-making
- Burnout accelerates, often to a breaking point

Addressing burnout (even temporarily):

- Therapy or coaching sessions: \$100–\$200/hour

- Cutting a day/week: temporary drop in production
- Investing in a better work culture: upfront effort, long-term payoff

The math is clear: prevention and recovery are cheaper than collapse.

Action Step: Create a "burnout prevention" line item in your budget. Think of it as emotional overhead.

Strategies for Reclaiming Your Energy and Protecting Your Finances

1. **Downsize Without Defeat**

- Reduce office hours strategically
- Raise fees instead of increasing volume
- Simplify procedures or cut low-margin services

1. **Outsource and Delegate**

- Hire a practice manager or consultant
- Train staff to handle more of what drains you

1. **Schedule Mini-Sabbaticals**

- One week every quarter completely off
- Use to reflect, recharge, travel, or reconnect

1. **Create a "Burnout Emergency Fund"**

- 3–6 months of personal and business expenses
- Gives you options if you need to pause or pivot

1. **Redefine Success**

- Not just numbers, but how you feel when you walk into your office

Action Step: Choose one burnout-busting strategy and schedule time this week to implement it.

What If You Want to Step Away Entirely?

Not everyone recovers and returns. Some dentists decide to:

- Sell their practice early
- Transition to teaching or consulting
- Work part-time only
- Switch careers entirely

Things to Consider:

- Practice valuation (get an expert)
- Tax consequences of a sale
- Health insurance if leaving employer coverage
- New income sources (real estate, investments, spouse's income)

Action Step: Create a "Plan B" document. If you needed to exit in 6–12 months, what would that look like?

Mental Health and Money Are Intertwined

Burnout can lead to:

- Depression
- Anxiety
- Poor decision-making
- Impulsive spending or avoidance behaviors

And financial stress can *cause* burnout, especially in:

- New grads with heavy debt
- Practice owners facing overhead pressure
- Mid-career dentists comparing themselves to peers

Action Step: If you're struggling emotionally, talk to a therapist who understands healthcare professionals. Don't wait until you're in crisis.

Designing a Financial Life That Supports Your Well-Being

Ask:

- Does my schedule allow me to rest?
- Do I have margin in my budget for self-care?
- Are my financial goals aligned with my real values—or just my peers' expectations?

Examples of Financial Decisions That Reduce Burnout:

- Moving to a smaller home with a lower mortgage
- Hiring more help at work
- Saving aggressively so you can reduce hours later
- Paying off loans early to free mental space

Action Step: Identify one financial change that could reduce your stress—even if it doesn't "optimize ROI."

Talk About It: Reducing the Shame Around Burnout

Dentistry breeds a culture of silence around struggle. But talking about burnout:

- Normalizes it
- Creates support networks
- Sparks creative solutions

Ways to Start the Conversation:

- Peer groups
- Study clubs
- Online forums
- With your spouse or advisor

Action Step: Share your experience with one trusted colleague. You might be surprised how much they relate.

Closing Thoughts: Your Health Is Your Greatest Asset

Burnout doesn't mean you're broken. It means you've been pushing too hard, for too long, with too little support.

You don't have to burn out to prove your worth. You don't have to hit rock bottom to make a change.

You can:

- Slow down
- Get help
- Change direction
- Rebuild with purpose

Your career is important. Your finances are important. But *you*—your joy, your health, your presence with your family—are more important.

So take care of you. The numbers will follow.

You've got this. And you don't have to carry it alone.

Chapter 27: Divorce and the Financial Fallout for Dentists

Let's begin with the truth:

No one walks down the aisle thinking about divorce. But life, as we know, can take turns we never expected. And when you're a dentist—someone who has built a business, carries substantial student debt, or owns real estate and retirement accounts—the financial aftermath of divorce can feel overwhelming.

This chapter is about helping you find clarity, steadiness, and smart strategy if you're navigating—or preparing for—the financial side of divorce. Whether it's happening now or something you want to plan against, this is your nonjudgmental, practical guide.

We're not here to point fingers or dwell on heartbreak. We're here to protect what you've built, give you tools to move forward, and remind you that this chapter of life doesn't define you.

You can recover. You can rebuild. And you can still thrive.

Why Divorce Hits Dentists Differently

Dentists are not like other professionals when it comes to divorce:

- You may own a practice—a complex asset that must be valued and potentially divided.
- You likely have student debt and business loans that muddy the picture.
- Your income may be volatile, especially early in ownership.
- You may have retirement accounts tied to both personal and practice

income.

In short: the stakes are high, and the details are tricky.

Action Step: If you're contemplating divorce, talk to a family law attorney and a financial planner *before* filing. Clarity now will save pain later.

Understanding Marital vs. Separate Property

One of the first questions in divorce is: What's shared and what's not?

Marital Property (typically shared):

- Income earned during the marriage
- Property or assets purchased together
- Contributions to retirement accounts during the marriage

Separate Property (typically not shared):

- Assets owned before marriage
- Inheritance received by one spouse
- Gifts given specifically to one person

But it gets murky fast, especially when:

- Separate assets are co-mingled with marital assets
- One spouse works in or helps with the dental practice

Real-World Example: Dr. H owned her practice before marriage but brought her spouse in to help with bookkeeping. After ten years, the court ruled part of the practice value was marital due to their joint efforts.

Action Step: Gather a timeline of when major assets and accounts were acquired. You'll need it.

Valuing a Dental Practice in Divorce

A practice isn't just a job—it's an asset. But how much is it worth?

Valuation considers:

- Revenue and profit (usually 3–5 years)
- Patient base
- Reputation and goodwill
- Staff and systems
- Location and lease
- Equipment and technology

Three common methods:

- Market approach (comps)
- Income approach (based on future cash flow)
- Asset-based approach (equipment, furniture, etc.)

Important Note: If the practice existed before marriage, part of it may still be marital if it grew significantly during the marriage or if your spouse contributed to it.

Action Step: Hire a certified practice valuation expert—preferably one who works with dentists and divorce attorneys.

Dividing Debt: Student Loans, Business Loans, and More

Debt division is just as important as asset division.

Student Loans:

- Usually considered separate if incurred before marriage
- May be considered marital if borrowed during the marriage and used for joint benefit

Business Loans:

- If the loan supports a practice that's considered marital property, it may be shared debt
- Collateral may include marital property

Credit Cards and Personal Loans:

- Shared cards are usually split
- Individual cards: depends on who used them and for what

Action Step: List all debts by:

- Who's listed on the debt
- When it was incurred
- What it was used for

This helps you and your attorney advocate for a fair split.

Spousal Support and Child Support

Spousal Support (Alimony):

- Based on income disparity, lifestyle, and length of marriage
- Often temporary to help lower-earning spouse transition

Child Support:

- Based on income, custody arrangements, and state-specific guidelines
- May include education, healthcare, and extracurricular costs

For Dentists:

- If your income fluctuates (e.g., collections-based), it's essential to document trends
- If you pay yourself through an S-Corp, underreporting W-2 income may backfire

Action Step: Work with your CPA to create accurate financial statements reflecting your true earning capacity—before any negotiations.

Tax Considerations in Divorce

Divorce changes your tax landscape.

Key issues:

- **Filing status:** You may no longer qualify for "married filing jointly"
- **Child tax credits:** Who gets to claim dependents?
- **Alimony:** Not deductible for the payer (as of 2019)
- **Retirement account division (QDROs):** Needed for tax-free splitting of 401(k)s or pensions

Action Step: Meet with a tax advisor experienced in divorce *before* signing any settlement. The IRS doesn't care what your decree says if the rules aren't followed.

What Happens to the House?

The home can be the biggest emotional and financial asset.

Options:

- One spouse buys the other out
- Sell and split the proceeds
- One keeps it temporarily (e.g., until kids graduate)

Considerations:

- Can you afford the home on one income?
- How will equity be handled?
- Who's responsible for mortgage, taxes, and upkeep?

Real-World Tip: Don't rush to keep the house "for the kids" if it jeopardizes your financial future.

Action Step: Get a current home appraisal and a realistic post-divorce budget before deciding.

Insurance: A Forgotten but Crucial Detail

Life Insurance:

- May be required to secure child or spousal support
- Review beneficiaries post-divorce

Health Insurance:

- If spouse was on your plan, they'll need COBRA or their own

Disability Insurance:

- Still critical—especially if you're now the sole provider

Action Step: Review all policies and update coverage, beneficiaries, and payment plans as soon as separation begins.

Rebuilding Your Financial Life Post-Divorce

The storm doesn't last forever. But rebuilding takes intention.

Steps to take:

1. Create a new budget based on your solo income and lifestyle
2. Revisit your retirement plan
3. Set new goals (home, career, travel, savings)
4. Rebuild credit if needed
5. Update all estate documents

Emotional Truth: It may feel like starting over—but you're starting wiser.

Action Step: Within 30 days of divorce finalization, complete a "Financial Reset Checklist" with your planner.

Closing Thoughts: You're Not Defined by Divorce

Divorce is a transition—not a failure. It's painful, yes. But it's also an opportunity to rebuild on stronger, wiser, more intentional ground.

You've worked too hard to let this chapter derail your future. You can:

- Protect your practice
- Rebuild your wealth
- Support your kids
- Reclaim your peace

So take a deep breath. Gather your team. Make each decision with clarity—not fear.

You've got this. And your next chapter can be brighter than you ever imagined.

Chapter 28: Managing Student Loans and Forgiveness Programs

Let's get real for a moment.

If you're a dentist, chances are student loans have shaped your financial life in some pretty big ways. Maybe you're carrying $200,000. Maybe it's $400,000 or more. Maybe it still makes your stomach tighten when you open your loan servicer's website.

You're not alone.

Dentistry comes with a unique combination of high income potential *and* high educational debt. And unlike some other professions, you often have to manage those loans while building a practice, supporting a family, or trying to catch up on retirement savings.

This chapter is here to give you more than just information—it's here to give you peace of mind.

We'll break down repayment strategies, forgiveness programs, refinancing pros and cons, and how to finally take control of your loans without letting them control you.

Whether you're just graduating or still chipping away after ten years, this is your map forward.

The Scope of the Problem: Why Dental School Debt Feels So Heavy

Let's look at the numbers:

- Average dental school debt in the U.S. now exceeds $300,000
- Many dentists attend private schools, where the total cost can approach

$500,000

- Interest accrues during school and often capitalizes after graduation
- Repayment starts at the same time you're trying to:
- Buy a home
- Get married
- Start a practice
- Pay for CE
- Save for retirement

Emotional Weight:

- Debt shame
- Guilt over interest
- Anxiety about never paying it off

Let's breathe. There are smart ways to manage this.

Action Step: Find your total current loan balance and average interest rate. Write it down. We're going to turn the unknown into the known.

Federal Loans vs. Private Loans: Know the Difference

Federal Loans:

- Direct Subsidized/Unsubsidized Loans
- Grad PLUS Loans
- Eligible for income-driven repayment (IDR) and forgiveness
- Flexible options (deferment, forbearance, PSLF)

Private Loans:

- Often refinanced loans
- Fixed or variable interest rates
- No forgiveness
- Less flexibility in hardship

Action Step: Make a list of all your loans. Separate federal from private. This matters for every decision that follows.

Option 1: Income-Driven Repayment (IDR)

Plans Include:

- SAVE (formerly REPAYE)
- IBR (Income-Based Repayment)
- PAYE (Pay As You Earn)

How It Works:

- Monthly payments are based on a % of your discretionary income
- After 20–25 years of payments, remaining balance may be forgiven
- Forgiveness is taxable (unless under PSLF—see below)

Pros:

- Lower payments in early years
- Payment scales with income
- Potential forgiveness

Cons:

- You may pay more in interest over time
- Forgiven amount may be taxed
- Long repayment timeline

Action Step: Use the Loan Simulator tool on studentaid.gov to compare IDR options based on your income and family size.

Option 2: Public Service Loan Forgiveness (PSLF)

Eligibility Requirements:

- Must work for a qualifying non-profit or government employer

- Must have Direct Loans
- Must be on an IDR plan
- Must make 120 qualifying payments

Perfect For:

- Dentists working in public health, VA clinics, community health centers, dental schools, or FQHCs

Pros:

- Full forgiveness after 10 years (120 payments)
- Forgiven amount is tax-free

Cons:

- Must stay in qualifying employment
- Paperwork and annual recertification are essential

Real-World Example: Dr. L worked for an FQHC and had $360,000 forgiven through PSLF. She made the minimum payment on SAVE for ten years while focusing on building savings and buying a home.

Action Step: If you're even *considering* PSLF, consolidate to Direct Loans and certify your employment annually.

Option 3: Refinancing

How It Works:

- Replace your federal or private loans with a new private loan at a lower interest rate

Pros:

- Lower interest rate

- Shorter repayment timeline
- Can save tens of thousands in interest if you repay aggressively

Cons:

- Lose federal protections (forgiveness, deferment, forbearance)
- Must have strong credit and high income
- Not ideal if your income is still variable

Good Candidates:

- Dentists in private practice or high-income associateships
- No intention of PSLF or other forgiveness
- Strong credit and emergency fund in place

Action Step: Shop rates with multiple lenders (Laurel Road, SoFi, Earnest, Credible) *but don't refinance until you're sure you won't need federal protections.*

Which Strategy Is Right for You?

Ask:

- What's my income now vs. projected income?
- Do I work in (or plan to work in) public service?
- How risk-tolerant am I?
- Do I have an emergency fund?
- Is tax planning part of my long-term strategy?

If you're early-career: IDR or PSLF often makes sense. **If you're mid-career and stable:** Refinancing can save money.

Action Step: Create a 10-year plan with your advisor: include projected income, family changes, home/practice purchase, and savings goals.

How Student Loans Impact Other Financial Goals

Buying a Home:

- IDR payments can lower your DTI (debt-to-income ratio) on mortgages
- Refinancing can help too, but increases minimum monthly payment

Starting a Practice:

- Lenders focus more on cash flow than debt total
- Student loans won't disqualify you—but repayment plan affects approval

Retirement Savings:

- Don't delay retirement savings until loans are gone
- Even small Roth IRA contributions compound massively over time

Action Step: Don't wait for forgiveness or payoff to build wealth. Save *something* for retirement now.

Mistakes to Avoid

1. Ignoring your loans for too long
2. Paying more than needed while on PSLF
3. Refinancing federal loans without understanding the trade-offs
4. Not recertifying IDR income annually
5. Not factoring loan payments into practice ownership planning

Action Step: Set a calendar reminder 60 days before your IDR recertification is due. Stay ahead.

Coordinating Loans with Your Tax Strategy

For IDR and PSLF, tax planning *matters*.

- Lower AGI = lower monthly payments
- Contribute to pre-tax accounts (401(k), HSA) to reduce AGI

Real-World Example: Dr. P maxed out her 401(k), HSA, and Dependent

Care FSA to reduce her AGI and lower her IDR payment by $600/month—saving $7,200/year.

Action Step: Work with a CPA who understands IDR plans and forgiveness. Tax and loans go hand-in-hand.

Divorce, Marriage, and Loans

Filing Jointly vs. Separately:

- Affects IDR payment calculation
- Filing separately can reduce your IDR payment, but may increase taxes

Spouse's Income:

- May be counted depending on your plan (SAVE vs. IBR)

Prenups and Loan Liability:

- Consider a prenup or postnup if one spouse has significant debt

Action Step: Before marriage or filing taxes, run the numbers both ways with a CPA and a student loan planner.

The Emotional Side: Getting Past the Shame and Stuckness

You are not your loan balance. You are not a failure because you borrowed for your education. You are not behind just because others are debt-free.

Reframe:

- This was an investment in a career that can produce $8–12 million over your lifetime.
- You have options.
- You can pay it off—or work the system toward forgiveness.

Action Step: Stop thinking in terms of "I owe $400k." Start thinking in terms of: "I pay $X/month, and here's what that enables me to do."

Closing Thoughts: Don't Let Debt Define Your Story

Student loans are part of your journey. They are not your finish line. You can:

- Own a home
- Build a practice
- Take vacations
- Save for retirement
- Raise a family
- Give generously

...and still have loans.

It's not either-or. It's about managing your loans wisely while building your life with intention.

You've got this. Let's keep going—strong, smart, and free from fear.

Chapter 29: Tax Strategies for High-Earning Dentists

Let's talk about something most dentists think about—but few truly plan for: Taxes.

When you're a high-earning professional, taxes can quietly become your biggest annual expense. And yet, too many dentists treat taxes reactively—only thinking about them when the year is already over, the return is being filed, and the damage is done.

This chapter is about flipping that script.

We're going to break down smart, proactive, and legally sound tax strategies designed specifically for high-income dentists in 2025. Whether you're an associate earning a healthy salary, a practice owner juggling payroll and equipment, or someone thinking about retirement, this chapter will give you clarity, options, and action steps you can take right now.

Let's start putting your money where it matters.

The 2025 Tax Landscape: What's Changed?

The IRS adjusts tax brackets, standard deductions, and contribution limits annually to reflect inflation—and in 2025, those numbers have shifted again.

Here's what you need to know:

Standard Deduction (2025):

- $15,000 for single filers
- $30,000 for married couples filing jointly

- $22,500 for heads of household

Top Federal Marginal Tax Rate: Still 37%, but the brackets have widened. That means more income is taxed at lower rates before you hit the top tier.

Key Retirement Plan Contribution Limits (2025):

- 401(k): $23,000 (plus $7,500 catch-up if over 50)
- Traditional/Roth IRA: $7,500 (plus $1,000 catch-up if over 50)
- HSA: $4,300 for individual / $8,650 for family (plus $1,000 catch-up if over 55)

Action Step: Update your tax prep checklist with 2025 limits. Every dollar of deferred income is a dollar not taxed today.

Strategy #1: Maximize Tax-Advantaged Retirement Contributions

One of the simplest, most effective strategies to lower your taxable income is to fully fund your retirement accounts.

If you're an employee:

- Max out your 401(k)
- Contribute to a Roth IRA (if under income limits) or consider a Backdoor Roth

If you own a practice:

- Open a Solo 401(k), SEP IRA, or Defined Benefit Plan
- Consider a cash balance plan for even higher contributions if you have steady profits

Real-World Example: Dr. K, a solo practice owner earning $400,000/year, contributes $69,000 annually to her defined benefit plan and $23,000 to her Solo 401(k), reducing her taxable income by $92,000. She's saving for retirement and cutting her tax bill simultaneously.

Action Step: Meet with a retirement plan specialist to model how much you can contribute based on your 2025 income.

Strategy #2: Choose the Right Business Entity Structure

If you're a practice owner, how your business is structured can have a major impact on your taxes.

Common structures:

- Sole Proprietorship
- LLC
- S Corporation

Why S-Corp often wins:

- You pay yourself a "reasonable salary" (subject to payroll taxes)
- Remaining profit can be distributed as dividends—not subject to self-employment tax

Caution:

- Must file payroll and run regular distributions
- IRS scrutinizes unreasonably low salaries

Real-World Tip: Many dentists use an S-Corp structure to save 5–7% in self-employment tax on a portion of their income—but it must be documented and compliant.

Action Step: Review your business structure with your CPA annually. The right fit may evolve with your income.

Strategy #3: Leverage Section 179 and Bonus Depreciation

Buying new equipment? Renovating your office?

You may be able to deduct the full cost in the year of purchase using:

- Section 179: Up to $1,220,000 in 2025
- Bonus Depreciation: 60% of qualifying assets in 2025 (phasing down from 100%)

Eligible items include:

- Dental chairs
- Imaging systems
- Computers and software
- Furniture
- Office renovations

Action Step: Time major purchases strategically. Buy in Q4? You may still get the full deduction.

Strategy #4: Hire Your Family Members

Have a spouse or teenage children?

- Hire them to do legitimate work for your practice
- Pay them a reasonable wage
- Wages are a deductible business expense
- Children under 18 employed by sole proprietors pay no FICA

Bonus:

- Kids can use income to fund a Roth IRA (tax-free growth!)

Action Step: Document job roles and hours. Pay via payroll like any employee.

Strategy #5: Use an HSA for Triple Tax Benefits

If you have a high-deductible health plan, HSAs are unbeatable.

- Contributions are tax-deductible
- Growth is tax-deferred
- Withdrawals for medical expenses are tax-free

Use it for future dental CE, vision, braces for kids—HSA money rolls over indefinitely.

Action Step: Open and fund your HSA before year-end to deduct it for 2025.

Strategy #6: Track and Deduct Business Expenses Carefully

Common deductions for dentists:

- CE and licensing fees
- Malpractice insurance
- Office supplies and uniforms
- Travel (if business-related)
- Meals with staff or vendors (50% deduction)

Be Cautious With:

- Vehicles (must track mileage carefully)
- Home office (if you're a practice owner working remotely)
- Commingled personal/business expenses (a red flag!)

Action Step: Use a dedicated business credit card and accounting software. Don't rely on memory come tax time.

Strategy #7: Invest Tax-Efficiently

Taxable brokerage account tips:

- Hold investments longer than 1 year to get long-term capital gains rates (0%, 15%, 20%)
- Use tax-loss harvesting to offset gains
- Favor ETFs (more tax-efficient than mutual funds)

Real-World Example: Dr. T sold a poorly performing stock at a $10,000 loss and used the loss to offset gains from selling real estate. He saved over $3,000 in taxes.

Action Step: Coordinate investment strategy with your tax planning—not after the fact.

Strategy #8: Consider Charitable Giving With Tax Benefits

Give with strategy:

- Donate appreciated stock instead of cash (avoid capital gains)
- Use a Donor-Advised Fund (DAF) to bunch donations into high-income years
- Consider QCDs if over age 70 1/2

Action Step: Work giving into your tax plan by Q4—not after New Year's.

Strategy #9: Plan for AMT and NIIT

Alternative Minimum Tax (AMT):

- Affects some high-income earners with large deductions

Net Investment Income Tax (NIIT):

- 3.8% surtax on investment income if income >$250,000 (MFJ) or $200,000 (single)

Strategies to mitigate:

- Defer income
- Increase pre-tax contributions
- Limit capital gains in affected years

Action Step: Run a projection with your CPA mid-year to assess exposure.

Avoiding Common Tax Mistakes

1. Waiting until March or April to think about taxes
2. Failing to pay estimated taxes quarterly (and incurring penalties)
3. Not adjusting withholdings or estimated payments as income grows
4. Not documenting deductions thoroughly
5. Choosing the wrong retirement plan for your practice structure

Action Step: Schedule a tax planning meeting with your CPA *before* October 15. Don't just file—plan.

Closing Thoughts: Taxes Don't Have to Hurt

Here's the thing: You're not just a dentist. You're also a business owner, an investor, a provider, and a wealth builder.

And taxes, when approached thoughtfully, can become a powerful part of your strategy—not just an expense.

You've worked too hard to leave money on the table. So take the next step:

- Plan ahead
- Work with great advisors
- Keep great records
- Maximize every dollar

You've got this. And with the right plan in place, your tax strategy can support the life and legacy you're building—on your terms.

Chapter 30: Teaching, Mentoring, and Giving Back

Let's close with something powerful. Something beyond spreadsheets, production goals, or practice valuations.

Let's talk about legacy.

At some point in your journey—maybe after paying off that last student loan, maybe after selling your practice, or maybe in the middle of an ordinary Wednesday—you'll start thinking about what it all means. About how to use what you've built to give back.

For dentists, this can take many forms: mentoring a younger colleague, teaching at a local dental school, offering free care to underserved communities, or even building a charitable foundation.

This chapter is about how to integrate meaning, mentorship, and generosity into your financial and professional life. Not someday, but now.

Because giving back doesn't just help others—it keeps you connected to your purpose.

Why Giving Back Matters in Dentistry

You've seen it. A colleague near burnout finds new life in mentoring. A retired dentist discovers joy again while teaching. A young dentist grows in confidence from a seasoned advisor's belief.

Giving back isn't a detour from your career—it's the next stage of it.

Benefits of giving back:

- Reignites passion and purpose
- Expands your professional legacy
- Strengthens the dental community
- Supports those who lack access to care
- Opens doors for underrepresented voices in the profession

Action Step: Think back—who helped you become who you are today? Make a list. What did they do that left a mark?

Mentorship: The Ripple Effect of One Conversation

Mentorship isn't just about formal programs. Sometimes it's a five-minute phone call. A lunch. A quiet vote of confidence.

Ways to mentor:

- Informal mentoring of younger associates
- Hosting shadowing students in your practice
- Being available for career questions online or via study clubs
- Creating a structured mentorship program within your group practice

Pros:

- Fosters leadership skills
- Keeps you learning
- Provides fulfillment
- Builds succession options for practice owners

Cons:

- Time-consuming if unstructured
- Emotional energy required

Real-World Example: Dr. F, after 25 years in practice, hosts a quarterly "Dinner and Dentistry" roundtable with local dental students. It's casual, real, and completely changed her relationship with the profession.

Action Step: Choose one person this month—a younger colleague, recent grad, or dental student—and offer to answer their questions over coffee. That's mentoring.

Teaching: Sharing Skills, Stories, and Systems

Teaching is one of the most overlooked ways for dentists to diversify their careers, extend their income, and give back.

Where dentists teach:

- Dental schools and residency programs
- CE courses (clinical, business, or specialty topics)
- Community college hygiene programs
- Online courses and webinars

Pros:

- Reinforces your knowledge
- Creates side income
- Builds your reputation as a thought leader
- Offers structure and purpose post-retirement

Cons:

- Requires prep time and presentation skills
- Pay may be modest in academic settings

Real-World Example: Dr. L teaches part-time at a university clinic on Fridays. It covers his living expenses in semi-retirement and lets him guide students through real-world challenges.

Action Step: Reach out to your dental school or local community college. Ask how you could volunteer, guest lecture, or apply as adjunct faculty.

Volunteering: Serving With Your Skills

You don't need to change careers or take a sabbatical to give back. Sometimes you just show up, tools in hand.

Places to serve:

- Mobile dental clinics
- Free dental days (Give Kids a Smile, Missions of Mercy)
- Church, temple, or nonprofit-based clinics
- International missions
- Local homeless shelters or veteran services

Pros:

- Deep impact
- Builds team spirit (if you include your staff)
- Restores purpose when burnout creeps in

Cons:

- Can be emotionally heavy
- Requires careful scheduling

Action Step: Pick one giving opportunity this year. Commit. Show up. You'll likely receive as much as you give.

Creating a Giving Plan: Aligning Generosity With Strategy

Start by asking:

- What causes matter to me?
- How much time or money can I give realistically?
- Do I want to give as a business, personally, or both?

Build your giving plan into your financial plan:

- Use a donor-advised fund (DAF)
- Budget a monthly giving line-item
- Offer scholarships to local students

- Sponsor a community event or nonprofit clinic

Action Step: Work with your financial planner to set annual giving goals that align with your cash flow and values.

Giving Back Through Your Practice

Your office isn't just a business—it's a platform for impact.

Ideas:

- Free cleaning days for kids or seniors
- Rounding up patient payments to support local causes
- Matching employee donations
- Featuring a "Charity of the Month"
- Partnering with local schools for oral health education

Real-World Example: Dr. M runs a "Smiles for Seniors" event every November. Her patients, team, and community look forward to it as a yearly tradition.

Action Step: Brainstorm with your staff. What giving initiative could your practice lead or host this year?

Succession, Legacy, and Mentorship Combined

When you're planning to sell or transition your practice, giving back can blend beautifully with business.

Ideas:

- Mentor your successor over 1–2 years
- Build in a community mission as part of the transition
- Leave part of practice proceeds to a cause you care about

Action Step: Include legacy and giving conversations in your practice transition planning. It's not just about price—it's about purpose.

Closing Thoughts: Purpose is the Ultimate ROI

You became a dentist to help people.

At every stage—from struggling student to seasoned owner—that core never changes. But how you express it evolves.

Giving back doesn't require millions. It requires intention.

Whether it's a check, a conversation, an hour of care, or a few words of wisdom—you have the power to impact lives.

And in doing so, you reconnect with why you started all this in the first place.

Your legacy isn't measured in production. It's measured in people.

So teach. Mentor. Give. Lead.

Not someday. But now.

You've got this. And someone out there is waiting for the encouragement only you can give.

Chapter 31: Lifestyle Design – Living Well Without Overspending

There's a moment that hits most dentists sooner or later.

Maybe it's after your third big CE course of the year. Or while staring at your latest American Express bill. Or during a quiet moment in your office when you realize: You've worked hard, earned well—and yet you still feel stretched.

Not just stretched financially. Stretched emotionally. Tired. Out of alignment with the life you thought dentistry would create.

This chapter is about designing a life that feels good and functions well—without constantly chasing or overspending.

Because it's entirely possible to live richly, travel well, enjoy beautiful things, take care of your family, and still build wealth. You just need a clear plan, a grounded mindset, and a lifestyle that's shaped by intention—not comparison.

Let's talk about how to live well as a dentist without living beyond your means.

What Is Lifestyle Design?

Lifestyle design means creating a personal and professional life that aligns with your values, goals, and ideal day-to-day experience.

It's not about denial or minimalism (unless that's your thing). It's about:

- Living with clarity
- Spending with intention

- Choosing what matters most
- Letting go of what doesn't

Key elements of lifestyle design:

- Financial sustainability
- Mental and emotional wellness
- Physical health and rest
- Time freedom
- Alignment with your values and purpose

Action Step: Take inventory. What are the 5 most important things in your life right now? Write them down.

Now ask: Does your spending and schedule reflect those things?

The Dentist Lifestyle Trap

Dentists often feel pressure to project success:

- A large home in the right neighborhood
- Luxury vehicles
- Private school tuition
- Designer wardrobes
- High-end travel

There's nothing wrong with any of those things. But they come with real costs—not just financial, but emotional.

Lifestyle inflation shows up like this:

- Income increases → lifestyle expands just as fast
- Saving rate stays the same—or decreases
- You feel "broke" at $250k/year because your spending always keeps pace

Real-World Example: Dr. A made $300,000/year but saved only $10,000.

His car leases, travel, and home upgrades made him feel successful—but he had no margin.

Action Step: Calculate your current savings rate (savings / gross income). Is it 15% or more? If not, where is the money going?

How to Reframe "Enough"

Most dentists were never taught how to define "enough." We only know how to chase "more."

Signs you're living without a clear definition of enough:

- You spend emotionally, then regret it
- You don't know what your lifestyle actually costs
- You're unclear on how much you need to retire comfortably

Reframe:

- Enough is not a dollar amount. It's peace of mind, flexibility, and joy.
- Define it. Own it. Revisit it as your life evolves.

Action Step: Answer this: What does "living well" look like for me—not Instagram, not colleagues, but me?

Budgeting for High-Income Professionals

The word "budget" makes most dentists cringe. But budgeting isn't about restrictions. It's about clarity.

Use a "Values-Based Budget":

- Spend freely on what matters most
- Cut ruthlessly on what doesn't

Categories to track (monthly or quarterly):

- Housing (aim for <25% of gross income)
- Transportation (total vehicle costs <10% of gross)
- Childcare/education

- Travel/experiences
- Personal development
- Business expenses
- Giving
- Savings/investing (aim for 20%+)

Tools: YNAB, Monarch Money, Tiller, Excel spreadsheet, or a financial advisor portal

Action Step: Track 90 days of spending. Use that data—not guesses—to adjust your lifestyle to match your values.

Spending Triggers and Emotional Habits

For many dentists, overspending isn't logical—it's emotional.

Common triggers:

- Burnout and stress ("I deserve this…")
- Envy or comparison
- Boredom
- Impulse (scrolling + spending)

Real-World Tip: Create a 48-hour rule. When you want to make a large purchase, wait 2 days. If you still want it, go ahead. Most impulse fades.

Action Step: Identify your top 2 spending triggers. Write them down. Build a coping plan (e.g., take a walk, call a friend, journal).

Aligning Big Purchases With Long-Term Plans

Ask yourself:

- Does this purchase align with my 5-year vision?
- Will this still matter in 12 months?
- Is this a want, a need, or an emotional fix?

Common big purchases to reconsider:

- Car leases (especially luxury models with poor ROI)

- Home upgrades that don't increase equity
- CE courses taken out of FOMO

Real-World Example: Dr. R wanted a second home but realized he hadn't fully funded his 401(k) in 3 years. He pivoted, maxed out retirement, and bought a rental property instead.

Action Step: For your next big purchase, draft a quick 1-page justification. See how it aligns with your goals.

How to Live Well (Truly) Without Overspending

Instead of...

- Luxury for status → choose quality and timelessness
- Constant upgrades → choose contentment
- Fancy dinners → host people at home with heart
- Flashy travel → design memorable experiences

Living well =

- Deep relationships
- Health and rest
- Purposeful work
- Margin and flexibility
- Peace of mind—not just peace of place

Action Step: Create a "Live Well" list. 10 things that make you feel truly alive, relaxed, joyful. How many of them cost money?

Designing a Sustainable Lifestyle That Grows With You

1. Create lifestyle ceilings—not floors

- Cap car, house, and lifestyle upgrades as a % of income

2. Automate savings and investing

- Save first, spend what's left—not the other way around

3. Build in fun—on purpose

- Budget for joy, not just bills. Fun is not failure.

4. Regularly review your financial picture

- Do a lifestyle audit each year

Action Step: Review your current fixed costs. Are you "locked into" a lifestyle that would stress you out if income dropped by 20%?

Letting Go of Comparison

Dentistry is competitive. You may feel pressure to keep up with colleagues who:

- Seem to take more vacations
- Drive luxury cars
- Expand their practices faster

But here's the truth: You don't know what's behind the curtain. Debt. Stress. Lack of savings.

Your life, your numbers, your peace.

Action Step: Unfollow 5 social media accounts that trigger comparison. Create a digital environment that supports your goals.

Living a Wealthy Life, Now and Later

Wealth isn't just retirement. Wealth is:

- Time to walk your kids to school
- Peace knowing your mortgage is manageable
- A paid-for car you love to drive
- Dinners at home with laughter
- The freedom to say "no" when needed

Real wealth = health, joy, impact, and options.

Action Step: Ask yourself: If I had all the money I needed, what would change about my daily life? Start building toward that now.

Closing Thoughts: You Don't Have to Sacrifice Lifestyle for Wealth—You Just Have to Design It

You don't need to feel guilty for wanting nice things. You don't need to cut everything to build wealth. You just need a plan.

A plan rooted in what *you* want. A plan that helps you live well—not just spend well.

You have options. You have earning power. You have a life worth designing.

So build it—on purpose.

You've got this. And your future self will thank you.

Chapter 32: Disability Insurance and Income Protection

Let's talk about a topic that no dentist wants to think about—but every dentist needs to plan for.

What happens if you can't work?

Not for a week. Not for a month. But for a year... or more.

What if an accident, illness, or injury takes you out of the operatory?

Your hands—your body—are your livelihood. Without them, the income stops, but the bills don't.

Disability insurance isn't glamorous. But it's one of the most essential building blocks of financial security for dentists.

This chapter is about understanding how to protect your greatest asset—your ability to earn an income—and how to do it in a way that's smart, affordable, and customized to your needs.

Because protecting your paycheck is protecting everything else you're working to build.

Why Dentists Are Especially Vulnerable

Dentists rely on fine motor skills, vision, posture, and stamina. Even a minor condition—a hand tremor, a back injury, a pinched nerve—can end a clinical career.

Add to that:

- Long educational timelines
- High student debt

- Income often tied to production
- Business ownership risk (for practice owners)

And you get a profession that has both a high need and a high risk.

Real-World Example: Dr. J was in a car accident at 36. No broken bones, but permanent nerve damage in her right hand. She could no longer drill with precision. Her career ended overnight.

Without disability insurance, she would've lost her home and filed bankruptcy.

What Is Disability Insurance?

Disability insurance is income replacement. If you become too sick or injured to work, it pays you a portion of your income.

There are two main types:

- **Short-Term Disability (STD):** Covers 3–6 months after an injury or illness
- **Long-Term Disability (LTD):** Kicks in after STD ends and may pay benefits for years or until retirement age

For dentists, **long-term, own-occupation** disability insurance is the gold standard.

Own-Occupation Coverage: What It Means and Why It Matters

Own-occupation means you're considered disabled if you can't perform the duties of your specific occupation—even if you could do something else.

Without it, you could be denied benefits if you're still "able" to do *any* work.

Example: Dr. C develops tremors and can't practice dentistry—but could teach. With own-occupation coverage, he receives full benefits *even if he chooses to teach.*

Action Step: Pull out your current policy (if you have one). Look for the words "own-occupation." If it's not there, talk to an agent immediately.

Key Features to Look For in a Policy

1. **True Own-Occupation** – Not "any occupation" or modified definitions
2. **Benefit Amount** – Aim for 60% of your gross income
3. **Benefit Period** – Ideally to age 65 or 67
4. **Elimination Period** – Typically 90 days (waiting period before benefits begin)
5. **Non-Cancelable and Guaranteed Renewable** – Premiums can't change if you pay on time
6. **Residual/Partial Disability Rider** – Covers partial loss of income if you can work but not at full capacity
7. **Cost of Living Adjustment (COLA)** – Increases benefits annually to keep up with inflation
8. **Future Purchase Option** – Lets you increase coverage as your income grows without new medical underwriting

How Much Does It Cost?

Expect to pay 1–4% of your income for a good long-term disability policy.

Variables that affect cost:

- Age
- Health history
- Tobacco use
- Gender (women pay more)
- Specialty (surgeons pay more)
- Elimination period and benefit period

Tip: The younger and healthier you are, the cheaper it is to lock in a policy.

Action Step: Get at least 3 quotes from agents who specialize in dentist coverage. Compare side-by-side.

Group vs. Individual Policies

Group Policies (through an employer or association):

- Lower cost

- Limited coverage (often capped)
- Not portable (you lose it if you leave the job)
- Often taxed if premiums are employer-paid

Individual Policies:

- More expensive
- Fully underwritten
- Portable (you own it)
- Tax-free if you pay premiums personally

Hybrid Approach: Many dentists stack group and individual coverage to maximize protection.

Action Step: If you have a group policy, find out:

- Coverage amount
- Definition of disability
- Whether it's taxable or not

Then fill gaps with an individual plan.

Business Overhead Expense (BOE) Insurance

If you own a practice, this is a separate policy.

BOE pays your practice's overhead if you become disabled:

- Staff salaries
- Rent and utilities
- Equipment leases
- Insurance premiums

It does NOT replace personal income.

Tip: This can preserve your practice's value while you recover or plan a transition.

Action Step: Practice owners: ask your advisor about BOE insurance.

It's one of the most overlooked tools for income protection.

Tax Considerations

- If *you* pay the premiums with after-tax dollars, benefits are tax-free
- If your *employer* pays premiums, benefits are taxable

Tip: For most dentists, it's worth paying the premium personally to receive tax-free benefits.

Action Step: Check how your policy is paid. Ask your CPA if you're unsure.

What Happens If You Never Use It?

Great! That means you stayed healthy. But it doesn't mean it was wasted.

Disability insurance isn't an investment—it's protection. Just like auto insurance or malpractice coverage, you hope never to use it—but you're grateful if you need it.

Return of Premium Riders may refund part of your premiums if unused—but usually at a higher cost. Do the math with your advisor.

Alternatives or Complements to Disability Insurance

Emergency Fund – Aim for 6–12 months of expenses **Practice Buy-Sell Agreement** – With a disability clause **Income Diversification** – Rental properties, royalties, other passive streams **Spousal Income** – Dual-income households have more flexibility

Tip: Insurance is Plan A. Diversified income is Plan B.

Common Mistakes to Avoid

1. Waiting too long to apply (rates rise with age and health changes)
2. Buying policies with vague definitions of disability
3. Underestimating how much income you need to replace
4. Forgetting to update coverage as income increases
5. Relying solely on group policies

Action Step: Schedule an annual insurance review. Update income, practice status, and goals.

Real-World Scenario: The Power of Protection

Dr. M bought a disability policy in dental school. Five years later, he was diagnosed with an autoimmune disease that slowly impaired his fine motor control. His policy kicked in when he dropped below 50% of clinical productivity. It covered his income until he transitioned to teaching.

He kept his house. Supported his kids through college. And lived without financial fear.

That's what this chapter is about.

Closing Thoughts: Secure the Foundation

Your income is the engine that powers every part of your financial life:

- Debt repayment
- Retirement savings
- Lifestyle upgrades
- Practice investments
- Family support

Disability insurance protects that engine. It doesn't stop bad things from happening. But it keeps your life from going off a cliff if they do.

Don't skip it. Don't delay it. Don't assume your current policy is good enough.

Protect what you've built—and what you're still building.

You've got this. And with the right protection, you'll keep going strong, no matter what comes your way.

Part 4: Mid-Career & Leadership Years

Part 4 of *Financial Literacy For Dentists* is where your career matures—and so do your financial decisions. These are the years where you're no longer just "in the game"—you're leading it. Whether you're a seasoned associate, a thriving practice owner, or stepping into new leadership roles in dentistry or your community, this section focuses on maximizing what you've built, avoiding burnout, and fine-tuning your financial strategy for long-term impact.

We begin by tackling the evolving complexities of mid-career income. With more money coming in, the stakes are higher—and so is the temptation to overspend or overextend. We break down how to recalibrate your budget, optimize savings, and continue building wealth without lifestyle creep eating away at your progress. If Part 3 was about growing your money, this part is about making your money more efficient and intentional.

Next, we explore what it means to lead—not just in your practice, but in your life. Topics include:

- Transitioning from technician to CEO: Managing your practice like a business
- Staff retention, leadership development, and creating a workplace culture that reflects your values
- Setting up systems that create time freedom and reduce your personal workload
- Tax strategy optimization with a CPA who understands dental-specific

deductions

We also dive into estate planning, succession planning, and advanced insurance strategies that protect your wealth and prepare for the unexpected. These years are the ideal time to formalize your legacy plan, whether that's setting up trusts, educating your kids about money, or establishing charitable giving structures.

This section includes:

- Financial strategies for dual-income households
- Navigating the costs of raising children or supporting aging parents
- How to mentor younger dentists and give back to the profession
- Preparing for eventual transitions: retirement, partnership changes, or selling your practice

By the end of Part 4, you'll not only have the tools to manage more wealth—you'll have the confidence to lead with purpose. This part is about aligning your money with your mission and ensuring the next chapters of your career and life are driven by strategy, not stress.

Chapter 33: The Business of Dentistry – From Chairside to Entrepreneur

Let's get one thing straight: dental school taught you how to treat patients—but not how to build a business.

You learned how to extract wisdom teeth, do crown preps, and restore implants. You probably didn't learn how to read a P&L, negotiate a lease, manage a team, market your practice, or make sense of payroll taxes.

That's where this chapter comes in.

Because at some point in your journey—whether you're a brand new associate or a seasoned owner—you'll realize that dentistry isn't just clinical. It's a business.

And if you want freedom, options, and real wealth, you have to start thinking like an entrepreneur—not just a provider.

Let's talk about what it really takes to go from chairside to CEO.

The Mindset Shift: You Are a Business Owner

Dentists often see themselves as caregivers first. And that's good.

But if you own a practice—or plan to—then you're also:

- An employer
- A leader
- A brand
- A strategist
- A risk manager

The moment you sign that lease or acquire a practice, your role shifts. And the sooner you embrace it, the sooner you can grow with intention.

Action Step: Start referring to your practice as a "business" in conversations. It's not ego—it's accuracy.

The Four Phases of Dental Entrepreneurship

1. **Associate** – You work for someone else. You build skills and earn a paycheck.
2. **Owner** – You buy or start your own practice. You manage risk and reward.
3. **Operator-Investor** – You delegate, scale, and run the business *through* a team.
4. **Exit Strategist** – You plan your transition, whether selling, scaling down, or stepping out.

You don't have to reach all four. But knowing where you are—and where you're going—will shape every decision.

Action Step: Identify your current phase. Write down your ideal phase in 5 years.

Starting or Buying a Practice: The Entry to Ownership

Starting from scratch:

- More freedom to design culture and layout
- Lower upfront cost (but slower to profit)
- Must build everything from zero (marketing, systems, patient base)

Buying an existing practice:

- Faster cash flow
- Built-in patient base and team
- Higher purchase price and potential legacy challenges

Key Numbers to Analyze:

- Collections
- Overhead percentage (aim for <65%)
- Active patient count
- Hygiene recall rate
- New patient flow

Action Step: If ownership is on your radar, start shadowing practice owners. Learn what you *don't* see from the outside.

Leadership and Culture: The Heart of the Practice

You can't scale chaos. Your culture will drive everything from staff retention to patient loyalty to daily energy.

Core leadership skills for dentists:

- Clear communication
- Empowering others
- Giving feedback
- Modeling accountability
- Hiring slowly, firing kindly but firmly

Culture Checklist:

- Does my team feel safe speaking up?
- Do we share wins and losses openly?
- Is our mission clear and lived out?

Action Step: Schedule a 1-on-1 with each team member quarterly. Don't wait for problems to surface.

Systems Over Stress: Build Processes That Run Without You

The secret to freedom is systems.

- Scheduling protocols
- Financial arrangements
- Insurance processing

- Marketing calendar
- Hiring and onboarding
- Daily/weekly team checklists

When systems run the practice, people don't have to guess. And you don't have to micromanage.

Action Step: Choose one system to improve this month. Document it. Train your team. Delegate.

Understanding the Numbers: Your P&L Is Your Report Card

Don't outsource understanding.

Key Financial Reports:

- Profit & Loss (P&L)
- Balance Sheet
- Cash Flow Statement
- Production by Provider
- Collection Rate
- Overhead Breakdown

Benchmarks to know:

- Hygiene should be 25–30% of total production
- Rent should be <6% of collections
- Staff wages: 25–30% of collections

Action Step: Review your P&L with a dental CPA. If you don't understand it—ask. Learning this will change your life.

Marketing and Growth: Attracting the Right Patients

You're not just in the teeth business. You're in the people business.

Marketing pillars:

- Website that converts
- SEO + Google Business Profile

- Online reviews and reputation
- Internal referrals and reactivations
- Community involvement

Growth Tips:

- Measure new patients per month
- Track ROI on marketing spend
- Focus on lifetime value, not just volume

Action Step: Create a simple monthly marketing calendar. Even 2 hours a week of focused effort makes a difference.

Team and Compensation: Attracting and Keeping Talent

Your team can make or break your practice.

What great teams want:

- Fair pay and clarity on roles
- Appreciation and feedback
- Opportunities to grow
- A leader who listens and leads by example

Compensation Strategies:

- Base pay + bonus tied to performance
- Regular reviews and raises
- CE stipends and benefit flexibility

Action Step: Survey your team anonymously. Ask what they love, what they'd change, and what would make them stay.

Legal and Compliance: Protecting Your Business

Don't wait until there's a lawsuit or audit.

Must-Haves:

- Employee handbook
- Updated legal entity (LLC, S-Corp)
- Proper contracts (associate, lease, vendor)
- HIPAA and OSHA compliance
- Business insurance (liability, cyber, overhead)

Action Step: Schedule a compliance check-up with a dental-specific attorney. Preventing risk is cheaper than repairing it.

From Chairside to CEO: Letting Go to Grow

You can't scale if you're doing everything yourself.

Delegate, automate, eliminate.

- Hire a practice manager
- Empower your hygienists and assistants
- Step back to work *on* the business, not just *in* it

Real-World Example: Dr. V worked four 10-hour clinical days. After hiring a manager and training an associate, she now works two clinical days and two CEO days—and grew collections 35% in 18 months.

Action Step: Identify one task you do weekly that could be delegated with training. Start the transition this month.

Exit Planning: The Final Chapter of Entrepreneurship

Whether you're 35 or 65, an exit plan brings clarity.

Types of exits:

- Sell to an associate
- Partner buy-in (gradual transition)
- DSO sale
- Merge or consolidate
- Wind-down with closure or asset sale

Consider:

- Valuation
- Tax planning
- Staff transition
- Real estate (sell or lease)

Action Step: Even if you're years away, ask: If I wanted to sell in 3 years, what would need to happen? That's your blueprint.

Closing Thoughts: You're Not Just a Dentist—You're a Leader

The dental chair may be your starting point. But entrepreneurship is where you create freedom.

Freedom of time. Freedom of purpose. Freedom to build something bigger than you.

You don't have to be perfect. You don't have to have all the answers.

You just have to lead with intention.

This business is yours to shape. Shape it wisely. And shape it well.

You've got this. And the future you're building—practice, team, legacy—is worth every step.

Chapter 34: Teaching Kids About Money (Even If You Never Learned It Yourself)

There's a moment in every parent's life where they look at their child and think, "I want to do this differently."

Maybe your parents never talked about money. Maybe they did—and it was all stress, shame, or silence.

But now, here you are. A dentist. A parent. Maybe a business owner. You've worked hard to create financial stability—and you're realizing that teaching your kids about money might be just as important as earning it.

This chapter is about how to start that conversation.

Even if you were never taught. Even if you still feel like you're figuring it out. Even if you're afraid you'll say the wrong thing.

Because the truth is, you don't need to be a financial expert. You just need to be present, intentional, and willing to grow alongside your kids.

Let's break down how to raise money-smart kids in a world that rarely teaches them.

Why Financial Education Starts at Home

Here's the thing: your kids are learning about money whether you talk about it or not.

They watch how you swipe your card. They hear how you talk about bills, taxes, or debt. They feel the stress when money's tight—or the peace when it's not.

So the question isn't, "Will they learn about money?" It's: "What story will they absorb?"

Your job is to replace confusion with clarity.

Action Step: Reflect on your own financial upbringing. What messages did you receive? What would you keep, and what would you change?

Start Early—But Keep It Age Appropriate

You don't need to talk about compound interest with a kindergartener. You don't need to lecture your teenager about Roth IRAs (yet).

Here's a simple guide:

Ages 3–6: Money as a Tool

- Let them hold and sort coins
- Play pretend store
- Use cash visibly when possible
- Teach basic values like saving and generosity

Ages 7–12: Earning and Choices

- Allowance tied to chores or contribution
- Introduce saving/spending jars or a clear bank
- Let them make small spending decisions—and learn from mistakes

Ages 13–17: Budgeting and Banking

- Open a checking account with a debit card
- Involve them in planning for purchases or family vacations
- Talk about needs vs. wants
- Introduce the concept of income, taxes, and investing

Ages 18+: Real-World Finance

- Credit scores and borrowing
- Paying for college or trade school
- Managing their own part-time income
- Setting goals for financial independence

Action Step: Choose 1 money conversation to have this week based on your child's age. Keep it short and positive.

Allowance: Yes or No?

Some parents love it. Others avoid it. The truth is, allowance can be a powerful teaching tool *if used intentionally.*

Options:

1. Fixed allowance (teaches budgeting)
2. Chore-based allowance (teaches earning)
3. Hybrid: base allowance + bonus for extra work

The key: Tie allowance to *values,* not just money.

Example: "In our family, we earn money by contributing to the household. We also give some, save some, and spend wisely."

Action Step: Set up a basic allowance system. Decide on amount, frequency, and expectations. Write it down.

Modeling Behavior: Your Habits Are the Real Lesson

Your kids will remember:

- How you talked about money
- Whether you fought or avoided it
- What you prioritized
- How you handled success and setbacks

Model what you want them to mirror:

- Budgeting openly ("We're saving for a trip—so we're eating out less this month.")
- Generosity ("Let's pick a cause to donate to as a family.")
- Mistakes ("I overspent here—next time I'll plan better.")

Action Step: Share one financial decision you made recently. Let your child see your process.

Teaching Tools and Activities

Books:

- "Money Ninja" by Mary Nhin (ages 4–8)
- "How to Turn $100 into $1,000,000" (ages 10+)
- "I Will Teach You to Be Rich" by Ramit Sethi (college-age and up)

Apps:

- Greenlight (kids debit card + app)
- FamZoo (family bank system)
- BusyKid (chores + allowance + investing)

Games:

- Monopoly (classic!)
- The Game of Life
- Cashflow for Kids by Robert Kiyosaki

Activities:

- Budget for a family night out together
- Set a savings goal and track progress visually
- Compare prices while grocery shopping

Action Step: Choose one tool or activity and schedule it this month.

Talking About Debt, Credit, and College

This one is big. Especially if you're still paying off your own student loans.

Be honest without burdening: "Yes, dental school was expensive. I'm still paying for it. But I also love what I do. I want you to understand what it means to borrow money, so you can make wise choices."

Teach them:

- Credit cards aren't free money
- Paying interest costs you more over time
- Loans are sometimes necessary—but should be approached with clarity
- You can recover from mistakes, but it's better to avoid them

Action Step: When your child sees you pay a bill, explain what it's for—and how credit works.

What If You're Still Learning Too?

Perfect. That makes you the ideal teacher.

Why? Because you'll approach it with humility, openness, and empathy.

Say things like:

- "I didn't learn this as a kid, but I want to learn it with you."
- "I'm reading a book on money. Want to read it with me?"
- "Let's ask our advisor this question together."

Your growth gives them permission to learn, too.

Action Step: Pick a book, podcast, or video series to learn from together. Commit to 15 minutes a week.

Raising Generous Kids in a Material World

We want our kids to enjoy life. But also to appreciate what they have.

Ideas:

- Match their donations dollar for dollar
- Take them to volunteer events
- Encourage them to give time, not just money
- Talk about "enough" and gratitude

Real-World Example: Dr. N gives each of her kids $100 every December. Half must be donated or used for good. The kids research charities, talk about impact, and present their choices at dinner.

Action Step: Set a family giving goal this year. Let the kids help choose where it goes.

Legacy: Teaching Them What Wealth Really Means

Wealth isn't about money alone. It's about options, freedom, and values.

Teach your kids:

- That money is a tool—not a trophy
- That it can create comfort, freedom, and impact
- That being wealthy includes time, relationships, and health

Action Step: At dinner or bedtime, ask: "What does being rich mean to you?" Their answers will surprise you—and guide the lessons ahead.

Closing Thoughts: You're Already Doing It

The fact that you care about teaching your kids money? That's everything.

You don't need to know it all. You don't need to do it perfectly.

You just need to show up, start talking, and keep learning.

Because the best financial education happens in real life. In the grocery aisle. At the dinner table. On vacation. In moments that seem small—but shape everything.

So give yourself grace. Give your kids guidance. And give your family a legacy of wisdom, not just wealth.

You've got this. And your kids? They're lucky to have you.

Chapter 35: Branding, Side Hustles, and Monetizing Your Expertise

Let's start with a question most dentists don't ask themselves often enough:

What else do you know how to do?

You've trained for years to become a dentist—but that doesn't mean your value stops at the operatory. Your skills, stories, and insights have real-world value far beyond fillings, crowns, and clinical codes.

In today's world, your knowledge is your brand.

Whether you realize it or not, you are a brand. The way you lead your team, talk to patients, show up in your community, and speak online—that's all branding.

This chapter is about how to own that brand with intention. It's about finding meaningful, aligned, and profitable ways to take what you know—and turn it into something more.

A side hustle. A second income stream. A creative outlet. A legacy project.

Because wealth isn't just about what you earn in the chair. It's about the assets you create with your mind, your message, and your momentum.

Step One: Know What You Bring to the Table

Let's take inventory.

What do people always ask you about? What clinical skills do you excel at? What business or leadership lessons have you learned? What stories, struggles, or solutions do you have that others would value?

Examples:

- Clinical teaching: case studies, CE, workshops
- Business: systems, hiring, practice culture
- Personal: burnout recovery, motherhood in medicine, minority mentorship

Action Step: List 5 areas where you have deep experience or unique insight. These are potential brand anchors.

What Is a Personal Brand (and Why Dentists Need One)?

Your brand is your reputation. It's how people experience you—online and offline. It's what comes up when someone Googles you.

And in the age of social media, reputation spreads faster than ever.

Why it matters:

- Helps you stand out in a crowded market
- Attracts opportunities (speaking, writing, consulting)
- Builds trust with patients and peers
- Increases your value if you sell your practice

Branding isn't self-promotion. It's value communication.

Action Step: Google your name + "dentist." What shows up? What story does it tell?

Building Your Online Presence

You don't need to be a TikTok star. But you *do* need to be visible in the ways that align with your message.

Basic Platforms to Consider:

- LinkedIn: professional, B2B
- Instagram: visuals, lifestyle, quick tips
- YouTube: deep dives, tutorials, case breakdowns
- Blog: thought leadership, SEO

Choose ONE to start.

- Post once a week.
- Provide value: education, insight, inspiration.
- Show your face. Share your voice.

Action Step: Claim your handle on the platform that fits your comfort zone. Make one introductory post.

Side Hustles That Fit the Dental Life

1. Clinical Education

- Speak at conferences
- Host CE events
- Create online courses (Teachable, Kajabi)
- Write case reports or journal articles

2. Consulting

- New practice startups
- Team training
- Operations and systems

3. Product Creation

- Dental tools or tech
- Patient education products
- Practice management software

4. Content Creation

- Podcasting
- YouTube channel
- Social media influencer (authentically)

- Dental humor, lifestyle, or storytelling

5. Writing and Publishing

- E-books
- Articles for dental publications
- Children's books on oral health

6. Coaching and Mentorship

- Young dentist guidance
- Residency prep
- Burnout coaching

Action Step: Choose one category that resonates. Brainstorm 3 potential projects.

Monetization Basics: How to Turn Value Into Income

Online Course Example:

- $99 course on managing dental anxiety
- 200 purchases = $19,800 revenue

Coaching Model Example:

- $500/month coaching package for new grads
- 5 clients = $2,500/month extra income

Blog/YouTube Example:

- Ad revenue, affiliate links, product promotion

Important: Monetization should always follow trust-building. Serve first. Sell second.

Action Step: Sketch a simple value ladder:

- Free content (social, blog)
- Low-ticket offer (ebook, webinar)
- Mid-tier (course, consulting)
- High-ticket (speaking, coaching)

Time Management: How to Do It Without Burning Out

You're busy. The key to side hustles isn't doing *more*. It's doing *smarter*.

Tips:

- Block 2–3 hours/week for focused creative work
- Batch content creation (record 4 videos in one sitting)
- Outsource tasks (editor, VA, designer)
- Align projects with your passion to keep it fun

Real-World Example: Dr. T records one podcast episode per week, early Saturday morning. It's grown into a six-figure brand with sponsors and speaking gigs.

Action Step: Audit your weekly schedule. Where is there 90 minutes you could repurpose?

Legal and Financial Considerations

Treat your side hustle like a business.

Steps to protect yourself:

- Register an LLC (talk to your CPA)
- Separate business bank account
- Keep track of expenses and revenue
- Understand self-employment taxes
- Get contracts and copyright protections as needed

Action Step: If you've earned more than $600 from a side project, talk to a tax pro this quarter.

Dealing With Fear, Doubt, and Imposter Syndrome

Most dentists don't struggle with *ability*. They struggle with *visibility*.

"What if people think I'm showing off?" "What if I fail?" "What if I'm not an expert?"

Flip it:

- What if someone needs your story?
- What if this changes your future?
- What if this creates freedom you never thought possible?

Courage builds confidence—not the other way around.

Action Step: Write down your biggest fear. Now write a positive "what if" that flips it on its head.

Legacy and Long-Term Thinking

A brand is more than a hustle. It's a legacy tool.

Your voice, your lessons, your name—they can live beyond you.

A course can run while you sleep. A book can inspire someone 10 years from now. A video can shape a student who's never met you.

This is how you build income AND impact.

Action Step: Define your "why." Why do you want to share your message? What do you hope it leads to?

Closing Thoughts: You're More Than a Title

You're not just Dr. So-and-So. You're a thinker. A builder. A teacher. A creator.

You have insights people need. And you have more to offer than a chairside appointment.

So start where you are. Start small. Start scared, if you have to.

Just start.

You've got this. And the world—dentistry and beyond—is waiting to hear what you've got to say.

Chapter 36: Understanding How Dentists Get Paid – Fees, Contracts, and Equity

Let's have the real talk.

You spent years—decades, maybe—learning how to care for teeth. But no one ever taught you how you'd actually get paid.

Whether you're an associate, a partner, or a practice owner, understanding your compensation structure is essential—not just to avoid burnout, but to build a future that works for you.

This chapter breaks down how dentists earn income, what those numbers mean behind the scenes, and how to negotiate, track, and maximize your earnings. We'll walk through common pay models, hidden traps in contracts, and how equity can play a role in long-term wealth building.

Because when you understand the game, you can stop feeling like you're getting played.

The Core Three: How Dentists Make Money

Let's simplify it:

1. **Fees** – What you're paid per procedure or hour
2. **Contracts** – Agreements that define how and when you're paid
3. **Equity** – Ownership stakes that generate long-term value

The blend of these determines your cash flow, taxes, and wealth trajectory.

Action Step: Identify your current primary income stream. Write out what percentage of your total income comes from fees, contracts, or ownership.

Fee-For-Service (FFS): Control and Complexity

What it is: You set your own fees and patients pay you directly (often with reimbursement from their insurance).

Pros:

- Higher potential income per procedure
- Full control over fees and schedule
- Greater patient loyalty and retention

Cons:

- Requires strong marketing and patient communication
- Often slower collections
- Limited by what patients can/will pay out of pocket

Example: Dr. M runs a boutique FFS practice in a high-income area. His per-patient revenue is higher, but he spends more on marketing and patient education.

Action Step: If you're FFS, do a fee audit. Are your prices aligned with your local market and value?

Insurance-Driven Models (PPO/HMO): Volume and Negotiation

What it is: You agree to accept lower fees from insurance companies in exchange for access to their patient base.

Pros:

- Steady patient flow
- Easier marketing (patients come through plans)
- Predictable service volume

Cons:

- Lower reimbursements
- Delayed payments
- Less freedom to set pricing

Tip: Learn how to analyze PPO contracts. You may be losing more than you think.

Action Step: Ask your team to run a report: top 5 insurances, % of patients covered, and average write-offs per plan.

Associate Compensation: Salary, Percentage, or Hybrid?

Common Models:

1. **Straight Salary** – Guaranteed pay regardless of production
2. **Percentage of Production or Collections**
3. **Daily Rate + Bonus**
4. **Base Salary + Commission**

Pros of Fixed Pay:

- Predictability
- Great for new grads or slow seasons

Pros of Commission-Based:

- Unlimited upside
- Motivates efficiency

Watch for:

- Collection delays (your commission might be delayed if based on collections)
- Lab fee deductions (some practices pass these on to associates)
- Non-compete clauses

Action Step: Pull out your contract. What are you actually getting paid *on*—production, adjusted production, or collections?

Understanding Contracts: What to Watch For

Your compensation doesn't live in the procedures—it lives in the paperwork.

Key contract elements:

- Pay structure
- Benefits (malpractice, CE, health insurance)
- Term length and renewal conditions
- Termination clauses
- Restrictive covenants (non-compete, non-solicit)

Negotiation Tip: Always ask to see a sample monthly statement or production report *before* signing.

Action Step: Hire a dental-specific contract attorney for any offer review. It's worth every dollar.

Partnership and Equity Models

What is equity? Equity = ownership. You receive a portion of the profit (not just salary) and/or build value in the business over time.

Types:

- Fixed equity (buy-in once, receive distributions)
- Earn-in (grow your share based on performance)
- Phantom equity (profit share without legal ownership)

Pros:

- Long-term wealth
- Control over business decisions
- Passive income if structured well

Cons:

- Buy-in cost (can be high)
- Risk if practice declines
- Responsibility for liabilities

Action Step: If you're considering equity, get a valuation. Understand what you're buying—not just what you're earning.

DSO Models: Consolidation and Caution

What is a DSO? A Dental Service Organization provides back-end support (billing, HR, marketing) and may own or manage multiple practices.

Common arrangements:

- Employed by a DSO (fixed salary + bonus)
- Partner with a DSO (retain partial ownership)

Pros:

- Administrative relief
- Access to capital and tech
- Scalable career path

Cons:

- Loss of autonomy
- Pressure to hit metrics
- Reduced long-term ownership potential

Action Step: If approached by a DSO, ask: What happens to *your* income and control in year 3, 5, and 10?

Special Situations: Income Outside the Operatory

Examples:

- Teaching and speaking fees
- Online courses and CE content

- Consulting or coaching
- Real estate tied to your practice
- Investing in other dental ventures

Tip: These streams can stabilize your income during slow months or career transitions.

Action Step: Brainstorm one income stream you could develop outside of clinical dentistry in the next 12 months.

The Tax Impact of How You Get Paid

W-2 (Employee):

- Taxes withheld
- Limited deductions
- Simpler filing

1099 (Independent Contractor):

- Responsible for your own taxes
- Can deduct business expenses
- Must pay self-employment tax (15.3%)

Owner (S-Corp, LLC):

- Flexible salary/distribution structure
- More advanced tax strategies available
- Requires bookkeeping and quarterly payments

Action Step: Meet with a CPA to assess whether your current structure matches your goals and income level.

Tracking Your True Compensation

Don't just look at your paycheck. Look at:

- Gross production

- Net collections
- Adjustments/write-offs
- Lab and supply costs
- Time worked vs. income earned

Goal: Understand your *effective hourly rate* after all factors.

Action Step: Create a spreadsheet. Track monthly collections vs. hours worked. What's your real hourly value?

Red Flags and Traps to Avoid

- No written contract (verbal agreements don't hold)
- No clarity on how bonuses are calculated
- Non-compete clauses that limit future options
- Being paid on "net production" without understanding the deductions
- Signing equity deals without valuations

Action Step: Before signing *anything,* ask for:

- Production reports
- Fee schedules
- Prior associate compensation examples

Closing Thoughts: Understand It. Own It. Negotiate It.

You're not just working *in* dentistry. You're working *for* your future.

And every dollar you earn—or don't earn—adds up over time.

So read the contracts. Ask the questions. Know the numbers.

Because your income isn't just about effort. It's about *structure.*

You've got this. And when you understand how you get paid—you can finally get paid *what you're worth.*

Chapter 37: Culture and Cash – How Your Background Shapes Your Money Mindset

Let's take a step back from spreadsheets. From retirement projections and production goals.

Let's talk about something deeper—something most financial books ignore.

Your money mindset.

Because no matter how much you earn, how many practices you own, or how fancy your CE certificates are...

You still carry stories. Stories about what money means.

Stories from your childhood. From your family. From your culture. From your neighborhood, your education, your faith, your trauma, and your triumphs.

This chapter is about naming those stories. Not to shame them—but to understand them.

Because when you understand *why* you do what you do with money, you gain power.

Power to change. Power to grow. Power to lead your life, and your finances, with clarity and peace.

Where It All Begins: Your First Financial Classroom

We all had one. It was called *home.*

You may have grown up in:

- A household where money was scarce
- A home where success was flaunted
- A family that never talked about money
- A culture where wealth meant security
- A religion where wealth felt shameful

Whatever it was, it shaped your financial default settings.

Action Step: Think back to age 10. What was the tone around money in your home? What words were used? What feelings do you still carry?

Money Scripts: The Stories Running the Show

Brad Klontz, a psychologist and financial planner, coined the term "money scripts"—core beliefs formed early that guide our adult behaviors.

Here are a few common ones:

- "Money doesn't grow on trees."
- "Rich people are greedy."
- "If I just work hard, I'll be okay."
- "I'll always be in debt."
- "I need to take care of everyone else first."

The problem? These beliefs often go unquestioned—even when they no longer serve us.

Action Step: Write down one money belief you absorbed early. Ask: Is it always true? Is it helping or hurting?

Culture, Community, and Cash

Our cultural backgrounds shape:

- How we view saving vs. spending
- Our relationship with debt
- How we define success
- How we talk (or don't talk) about money
- Who we feel responsible for

Examples:

- Some cultures prize visible wealth—others value discretion
- Some emphasize collective support—others focus on independence
- Some reward generosity—others caution against giving too much

Real-World Example: Dr. R, a second-generation immigrant, sends 20% of her income back home to family. She felt guilty investing for herself—until she reframed it as legacy building *for* her entire family.

Action Step: Journal: What did your culture teach you about money that still guides you today?

Shame, Scarcity, and Survival Mode

Many dentists came from humble beginnings.

Maybe you:

- Watched parents live paycheck to paycheck
- Felt embarrassed at school because of hand-me-downs
- Were told to always save—but never taught how to invest

That survival wiring doesn't just disappear when your income increases.

Symptoms of financial trauma:

- Hoarding cash out of fear
- Avoiding investing
- Guilt about success
- Undercharging or overgiving
- Conflict avoidance in financial conversations

Action Step: Name the emotion. When you think about money today, is it fear? Guilt? Control? What's behind that?

Rewriting the Script: A New Money Narrative

You don't have to repeat the past. You don't have to reject it, either.

You get to rewrite the story.

From: "I'm not good with money." **To:** "I'm learning to manage my money with clarity."

From: "Money causes stress." **To:** "Money can be a tool for peace and impact."

From: "I never learned this." **To:** "I get to be the one who changes the pattern."

Action Step: Write one empowering sentence about money that you want to live by. Put it somewhere you'll see it often.

Generational Wealth: Building What You Didn't Have

If you're the first in your family to:

- Become a dentist
- Own a business
- Build a 401(k)
- Buy life insurance
- Plan an estate

You are *breaking cycles.* And that's hard. And lonely. And powerful.

You're not just building wealth. You're building *language.* You're building *confidence.* You're building *options* for the next generation.

Action Step: Write a note to your future child, grandchild, or mentee. Tell them what you're building—and why.

When Mindset Meets Money Decisions

Let's say you:

- Avoid investing because your parents lost money in 2008
- Overspend to feel successful after years of struggle
- Underpay yourself because you equate service with sacrifice

Those are mindset issues showing up in financial decisions.

Practical tools to shift:

- Therapy or financial coaching

- Journaling before big money decisions
- Regular money check-ins with a trusted advisor
- Money dates with your partner

Action Step: Choose one behavior you want to change. Write down the belief behind it. Replace it with a new one.

Leading with Financial Self-Awareness

If you're a practice owner, your mindset affects your team:

- How you talk about bonuses
- How you handle salary negotiations
- How you model abundance or anxiety

If you're a parent, your mindset affects your kids:

- What they think is "normal"
- What they feel safe asking about
- What they grow up repeating

Action Step: Before your next money conversation—with a staff member, spouse, or child—pause. Ask: What mindset am I bringing into this?

You're Not Behind. You're Becoming.

So many dentists feel like they "should" be further along. But maybe you're the first in your family to even have *this* opportunity.

Give yourself credit. Give yourself permission. Give yourself space to grow.

You're not broken. You're not late. You're learning.

And your financial life can be as intentional, beautiful, and grounded as the one you create for your patients.

Closing Thoughts: You Carry More Than Numbers

You carry history. You carry resilience. You carry the opportunity to do things differently.

And that? That's powerful.

So keep earning. Keep building. Keep healing your relationship with money.

Because when you heal your money story, you don't just change your life. You change everything downstream.

You've got this. And the wealth you're building? It's not just about the dollars. It's about who you're becoming—and what you're passing on.

And that is worth everything.

Chapter 38: Can You Manage Your Own Investments?

Let's start with the question at the heart of this chapter:

Can you manage your own investments?

The short answer? Yes.

The better question?

Should you manage your own investments?

That depends.

Because managing your own portfolio isn't just about saving fees. It's about knowing your temperament, your time, and your tolerance for complexity.

Some dentists thrive with a DIY approach. Others realize that managing crowns and managing capital require very different muscles.

This chapter will help you figure out where you fall—and how to move forward wisely, whether you're going solo or partnering with a professional.

The Case for DIY: Why Some Dentists Manage Their Own Money

Dentists are smart, capable, and often entrepreneurial. You've already built a career with precision and discipline—why not your portfolio?

Advantages of DIY Investing:

- Lower fees (no advisor management fees)
- Full control over asset allocation
- Greater financial literacy over time
- Customization to your risk and goals

Real-World Example: Dr. A reads investment books, listens to finance podcasts, and uses a robo-advisor platform to manage her retirement accounts. She reviews quarterly and rebalances annually.

Action Step: Reflect—do you enjoy learning about markets, strategy, and financial planning? If so, you might be a good candidate for DIY.

The Risks of Going It Alone

1. Behavioral Biases:

- Panic selling in downturns
- Chasing hot stocks or trends
- Overconfidence in timing the market

2. Time Constraints:

- Running a practice is already demanding
- Investment management adds hours of research and monitoring

3. Complexity:

- Tax-efficient investing
- Diversification across account types (taxable, IRA, Roth, 401(k))
- Estate planning and asset protection

Real-World Example: Dr. T tried day trading between patients. After a rough earnings season and a missed margin call, he lost $50K in a week. He now uses a hybrid model with an advisor.

Action Step: Audit your schedule. Do you realistically have 5–10 hours per month to dedicate to research, monitoring, and rebalancing?

What DIY Really Looks Like

If you're serious about doing it yourself, here's what you need:

Tools:

- A brokerage account (Fidelity, Schwab, Vanguard, etc.)

- A retirement account (401(k), IRA, Solo 401(k), SEP IRA)
- A budgeting app (YNAB, Mint, Monarch)
- Asset allocation plan

Knowledge Areas:

- Index funds vs. active funds
- Risk tolerance assessment
- Tax-loss harvesting
- Rebalancing schedule

Key Rule: Keep it boring. Boring makes money.

Example Portfolio (Age 35, Moderate Risk):

- 60% Total U.S. Stock Index
- 20% Total International Stock Index
- 20% Bond Index Fund

Action Step: Choose one platform. Set up a diversified, low-cost portfolio. Automate your contributions.

The Power of Simplicity: Bogleheads, Lazy Portfolios, and Indexing

You don't have to pick stocks to manage your own investments.

The Boglehead Philosophy:

- Invest in low-cost index funds
- Diversify globally
- Stay the course through market cycles
- Don't try to time the market

Sample Lazy Portfolio (3-fund):

- U.S. Total Market Index (VTI or equivalent)
- International Total Market Index (VXUS or equivalent)

- Bond Aggregate Index (BND or equivalent)

Why it works:

- Minimal fees
- Minimal trading
- High diversification

Action Step: Read "The Bogleheads' Guide to Investing." If you nod the whole way through, DIY might be right for you.

When to Hire Help (And How to Vet Them)

Signs you should consider an advisor:

- You hate dealing with investments
- You don't know what questions to ask
- Your portfolio is growing—and so are your worries
- You want holistic planning (taxes, estate, insurance, practice exit)

How to choose a good advisor:

- Fee-only (no commissions)
- Fiduciary (legally required to act in your best interest)
- Dental-specific experience is a plus
- Transparent, values-aligned

Questions to ask:

- How do you get paid?
- What services are included?
- Can I see a sample financial plan?
- What's your investment philosophy?

Action Step: Interview 2–3 advisors. Compare fees, style, and support.

Go with the one who makes you feel most empowered—not the one selling the most products.

Hybrid Models: The Best of Both Worlds?

Some dentists want control—but also want support.

Enter the hybrid model:

- DIY daily execution + annual advisor review
- Robo-advisor for simplicity + human check-ins
- Flat-fee planning without asset management

Pros:

- You save on fees
- You gain clarity
- You avoid decision fatigue

Example: Dr. P runs his own index portfolio but meets with a planner quarterly to review progress, taxes, and insurance.

Action Step: If DIY feels too risky, but full-service feels too expensive—look for a planner who offers one-time or project-based work.

Common Mistakes of DIY Dentists

1. **Neglecting rebalancing** – Portfolios drift over time
2. **Overtrading** – Activity doesn't equal returns
3. **Ignoring taxes** – Capital gains and asset location matter
4. **No withdrawal plan** – Retirement needs a decumulation strategy
5. **Paralysis by analysis** – Perfectionism keeps you stuck

Action Step: Choose one mistake you've made. Learn how to fix it. Make a note to check in every 6 months.

How Investment Management Ties to Your Life Plan

Your portfolio isn't a standalone project. It's a tool to:

- Retire early
- Pay for your kids' college
- Expand your practice
- Take time off without stress
- Give generously

Whether you DIY or hire help, keep your goals front and center.

Action Step: Write your top 3 life goals. Then, match your investment strategy to those priorities.

Closing Thoughts: Control Isn't Everything—Clarity Is

The truth?

You *can* manage your own investments. But that doesn't mean you have to.

You're not more "smart" or "worthy" because you DIY. And you're not weak if you ask for help.

What matters is that you:

- Understand your goals
- Know your limits
- Choose a path that fits your life, not someone else's opinion

You've got this. Whether it's through Vanguard or a financial planner's office. Because at the end of the day, investing isn't about complexity. It's about clarity.

And you deserve a financial future that's aligned, empowered, and built on purpose—not pressure.

Start where you are. Grow as you go. And build the kind of wealth that feels right—not just looks right.

Chapter 39: Opening and Managing an Investment Account

Let's talk about doors.

Because opening an investment account is like opening a door—to your financial future.

It's not just paperwork. It's not just a login screen. It's a gateway to autonomy, growth, and the kind of wealth that compounds quietly while you're helping patients, running your practice, or taking a much-needed vacation.

This chapter is your step-by-step walkthrough. Whether you're fresh out of dental school or well into your practice years, you'll learn how to open, fund, and manage your first (or next) investment account with confidence.

Let's break it down—clearly, simply, and practically.

Why Investment Accounts Matter (Even If You're Still Paying Off Loans)

Let's address the elephant in the operatory:

"Shouldn't I pay off my student loans before investing?"

It depends.

If your loan interest rate is low (say, below 5%) and you have a solid emergency fund, investing sooner—even small amounts—allows you to take advantage of time in the market.

Compound interest works best when given *years*, not just dollars.

And investment accounts give you access to that compound growth.

Types of Investment Accounts You Should Know

1. Tax-Advantaged Retirement Accounts:

- **Traditional IRA** – Pre-tax contributions, taxed on withdrawal
- **Roth IRA** – Post-tax contributions, tax-free growth and withdrawal
- **401(k)/403(b)/457** – Employer-sponsored, higher contribution limits
- **Solo 401(k)** – For self-employed dentists
- **SEP IRA** – For practice owners with few or no employees

2. Taxable Brokerage Accounts:

- No contribution limits
- More flexibility and liquidity
- Capital gains taxed, but can be managed smartly

3. Custodial Accounts (for kids):

- UTMA/UGMA – Gifts to minors that grow over time

4. 529 Plans:

- Tax-advantaged college savings

Action Step: Pick one account type you don't already have. Write it down. This week, research how to open it.

Where to Open an Account (and What to Look For)

Top online brokerage platforms:

- **Vanguard** – Low fees, long-term focus
- **Fidelity** – Great customer service, wide fund options
- **Charles Schwab** – User-friendly, good tools for beginners
- **Betterment/Wealthfront** – Robo-advisors, set-it-and-forget-it style

What to look for:

- No (or low) account minimums

- Low expense ratios on funds
- Easy-to-navigate platform
- Good customer support

Action Step: Choose one brokerage to explore. Create a demo account or review their site's FAQ.

The Actual Steps: How to Open Your First Account

1. Go to the brokerage website
2. Choose the type of account you want to open (IRA, taxable, 529, etc.)
3. Fill out basic info: name, address, Social Security number, employment status
4. Link a bank account to fund it
5. Select investment choices (or go with a target-date fund if unsure)
6. Review, submit, and confirm

Takes about 20–30 minutes start to finish.

Action Step: Block off 30 minutes on your calendar. Make this a real task.

How to Choose What to Invest In

If you want simple:

- A target-date fund based on your expected retirement year (e.g., 2065 fund)
- A robo-advisor that asks you questions and builds a portfolio

If you want more control:

- 60% U.S. total stock market index
- 20% international stock index
- 20% bond index fund

Golden rules:

- Diversify
- Avoid trying to time the market
- Keep fees low (expense ratios < 0.25% ideally)

Action Step: Write down your investing personality. Are you a hands-off delegator or an active learner?

What Happens Next: Funding and Rebalancing

Funding:

- Set up automatic monthly contributions
- Start with $100/month if that's all you can do

Rebalancing:

- Once or twice a year, check your allocation
- If stocks grew too much, sell a bit and buy bonds (or vice versa)
- Keep your portfolio aligned with your risk level

Action Step: Automate your contributions—even a small one. $100/month = $1,200/year without lifting a finger.

Tax Considerations

Taxable account:

- Dividends and capital gains may be taxed
- Hold investments longer than 1 year for long-term capital gains (lower rate)

Retirement accounts:

- Roth = tax-free withdrawals later
- Traditional = tax-deferred growth, taxed on withdrawal

Pro tip: Don't keep cash sitting in an investment account—invest it.

Action Step: If you're unsure what tax bucket to prioritize, talk to a financial advisor or CPA.

What to Watch For (and What to Ignore)

Ignore:

- Daily stock news
- Market predictions on CNBC
- What your cousin is investing in on Reddit

Pay attention to:

- Your goals
- Your savings rate
- Your portfolio's risk level

Action Step: Unsubscribe from hype-driven finance newsletters. Keep your focus long-term.

Real Dentist Stories

Dr. L set up her Roth IRA on a weekend. She used Vanguard's target-date fund and never looked back. Now, five years later, her account is thriving, and she's added a taxable brokerage account, too.

Dr. K started investing during his residency with just $50/month. He didn't understand everything at first—but he knew time mattered more than timing.

Dr. S waited 10 years because he felt intimidated. When he finally opened his 401(k), he realized it only took an hour—and regretted waiting a decade.

Common Questions

"What if I make a mistake?" You will. It's okay. Investing is a long game.

"Can I take money out if I need it?" Only from taxable accounts without penalty. Retirement accounts are meant for the long haul.

"Do I need thousands to start?" No. You can start with $50 or $100.

The key is starting.

Closing Thoughts: Your First Account Is a First Step

You're not behind. You're not too late. You're just ready now.

And that's more than enough.

Because every dentist who built wealth started with one step: Opening that account. Making that deposit. Choosing progress over perfection.

You've got this. And your investment account? It's not just numbers on a screen. It's the beginning of your future freedom.

Let's build it. One smart, intentional decision at a time.

Chapter 40: Advanced Investment Strategies – Risks, Rewards, and Cautions

By now, you've got the basics.

You've opened your investment accounts. You've picked your funds. You've automated your savings.

But if you're reading this chapter, it's probably because you're ready for more.

More growth. More leverage. More options.

This chapter isn't for everyone. It's not about keeping it simple. It's about understanding the advanced moves—the kind that can accelerate wealth, but also amplify risk.

It's about clarity, not complexity. It's about knowing what you're doing *before* jumping in.

So let's dig into advanced investing—strategically, not recklessly.

What Counts as "Advanced Investing"?

When we say "advanced," we don't just mean "risky."

Advanced means:

- Requires deeper knowledge
- May involve leverage or illiquidity
- Often used to reduce taxes or increase returns
- Usually involves more moving parts

Examples include:

- Real estate syndications
- Private equity
- Tax-loss harvesting and direct indexing
- Options and derivatives
- Venture capital and angel investing
- Alternative assets (art, wine, crypto)

Action Step: Write down why you're interested in going beyond the basics. Is it growth? Diversification? Tax savings? Make your "why" clear before your "what."

Real Estate Investing: Beyond Your Primary Home

You already know real estate can be a powerful wealth-builder. But there's more than just buying a rental down the street.

Advanced strategies include:

- Short-term rentals (Airbnb-style)
- BRRRR (Buy, Rehab, Rent, Refinance, Repeat)
- Real estate syndications (group investments)
- Real Estate Investment Trusts (REITs)
- Triple-net commercial leases

Pros:

- Tangible asset
- Tax benefits (depreciation, 1031 exchanges)
- Potential for cash flow and appreciation

Cons:

- Management headaches
- Liquidity risk

- Market and tenant variability

Real-World Example: Dr. M joined a dental-only real estate syndicate. She invested $50K, receives quarterly distributions, and gets tax advantages without direct property headaches.

Action Step: If interested in real estate, decide: Active or passive? Local or remote? Residential or commercial?

Tax Strategies: Harvesting, Location, and Asset Allocation

1. Tax-Loss Harvesting:

- Sell investments at a loss to offset gains
- Rebuy similar (but not identical) assets

2. Tax-Efficient Asset Location:

- Put high-growth assets (stocks) in Roth IRAs
- Put income-generating assets (bonds, REITs) in traditional IRAs or 401(k)s
- Use taxable accounts for tax-efficient ETFs

3. Tax-Optimized Withdrawal Strategies:

- Blend withdrawals from taxable, traditional, and Roth accounts to reduce lifetime taxes

Tools that help:

- Direct indexing platforms (e.g., Parametric)
- Advisors using custom allocation tech

Action Step: Ask your CPA or advisor: Are my investments tax-located efficiently?

Private Investments: Equity, Startups, and Alternatives

Dentists often get pitched deals—startups, dental technology, local businesses.

Before saying yes, ask:

- What's the business model?
- What are the risks?
- Who else is involved?
- What's my exit plan?

Pros:

- High upside potential
- Access to exclusive opportunities

Cons:

- High failure rate
- Long lock-up periods
- No secondary market (illiquidity)

Example: Dr. B invested $25K in a dental software startup. It failed within two years. He now requires pro forma financials and 3rd-party legal review before investing in anything.

Action Step: Create your "checklist" before saying yes to a private deal.

Options and Derivatives: Proceed with Caution

Unless you are:

- A trader
- A financial pro
- Deeply educated in market mechanics

...then options may be too risky.

Basic uses:

- Hedging
- Generating income via covered calls

Risks:

- Massive downside
- Time decay
- Complexity and leverage

Reality Check: If you can't explain the position in plain English, you probably shouldn't be in it.

Action Step: Stay out of options unless you've completed a certified course or practiced in a sandbox account for 6+ months.

Alternative Assets: Should You Invest in Art, Crypto, or Wine?

Everyone wants to diversify—but not everything is investable.

Alternative assets include:

- Crypto (Bitcoin, Ethereum)
- Art and collectibles
- Wine, watches, and memorabilia
- Sports card markets

Pros:

- Low correlation to markets
- Potential for high return

Cons:

- Illiquid
- Speculative
- No cash flow
- Hard to value

Action Step: Never put more than 5–10% of your net worth into alternatives.

Using Leverage: Margin, Loans, and Risk

Leverage = borrowing to invest.

Can be done via:

- Margin accounts
- Home equity loans
- Business loans reinvested

Pros:

- Amplifies returns

Cons:

- Amplifies losses
- Interest costs
- Margin calls (forced selling)

Real-World Story: Dr. Y borrowed against her home to invest in a friend's business. The business failed. She refinanced and now carries regret more than debt.

Action Step: Only use leverage when you fully understand the repayment plan and downside scenario.

Your Risk Tolerance vs. Your Risk *Capacity*

Risk tolerance: How much volatility you can stomach **Risk capacity:** How much risk your *life* can absorb

You might *feel* okay watching your portfolio drop 20%—but if you need that money for tuition, retirement, or debt repayment, you may not *afford* to lose it.

Action Step: Write down a worst-case investment scenario. Would it ruin you? Or just bruise your ego?

Working with a Financial Professional

Advanced strategies often require a team:

- Financial planner (CFP)
- CPA or tax strategist
- Estate attorney
- Investment analyst (optional)

The cost of advice is small compared to the cost of big mistakes.

Action Step: If you're using any strategy discussed here, set up a team check-in once a year.

Closing Thoughts: Sophistication Without Stress

You don't need complexity to build wealth. But if you *want* to go deeper—make sure it's grounded in:

- Your goals
- Your risk tolerance
- Your ability to focus and follow through

Don't chase status. Chase alignment.

Because the best investment strategy isn't the flashiest. It's the one that works for *you*.

So go smart. Go slow. Go informed.

And remember: advanced doesn't mean smarter. It means *intentional.*

You've built your dental career with precision, planning, and patience. Bring that same mindset to your investments.

Your future self will thank you.

Chapter 41: The Backdoor Roth IRA – How It Works and When It Makes Sense

Let's be honest—most dentists earn too much to contribute to a Roth IRA the traditional way.

And yet, the Roth IRA remains one of the most powerful long-term wealth-building tools available.

So how do you get in the back door?

That's exactly what this chapter is about.

The Backdoor Roth IRA is a legal workaround designed for high-income earners. It's a tax-smart move—but it must be done carefully. It's not for everyone, but for many dentists, it's an essential part of the retirement toolkit.

We'll cover how it works, who it's for, and what to avoid, with plenty of plain-English explanation and real-world dentist scenarios to make it practical.

Roth IRA Basics (Quick Recap)

A Roth IRA is a retirement account that:

- Uses *after-tax* contributions
- Grows tax-free
- Allows *tax-free withdrawals* in retirement (age 59.5+ and account open 5+ years)

2025 contribution limits:

- $7,000 per year ($8,000 if age 50+)

Income limits (2025, single filers):

- Begins phasing out at $146,000
- Ineligible above $161,000

Income limits (married filing jointly):

- Begins phasing out at $230,000
- Ineligible above $240,000

That's why most dentists need the backdoor.

What Is a Backdoor Roth IRA?

It's a two-step process:

1. Contribute to a traditional IRA (non-deductible)
2. Convert that contribution to a Roth IRA

No income limits apply to traditional IRA contributions or Roth conversions.

Key principle: The IRS doesn't limit Roth *conversions*—just Roth *contributions.*

So this strategy is 100% legal (and well-known among financial pros).

Step-by-Step: How to Do a Backdoor Roth IRA

Step 1: Open a Traditional IRA

- Any major brokerage (Fidelity, Vanguard, Schwab, etc.)
- Do *not* deduct it on your taxes

Step 2: Contribute to Traditional IRA

- Max for 2025 = $7,000 ($8,000 if 50+)

- Use post-tax money (from your checking account)

Step 3: Wait a few days

- Some advisors recommend waiting 1–2 days to avoid "step transaction" scrutiny

Step 4: Convert to Roth IRA

- Move the money from your Traditional IRA to your Roth IRA
- The sooner you convert, the less chance of taxable growth

Step 5: File IRS Form 8606

- This reports the non-deductible contribution and prevents double taxation

Important Caution: The Pro-Rata Rule

The biggest mistake dentists make with backdoor Roth IRAs? Ignoring the **pro-rata rule.**

If you already have other pre-tax traditional IRA funds, your conversion will be partially taxable.

Example:

- You contribute $7,000 post-tax
- You already have $93,000 in a pre-tax IRA
- Your total IRA balance = $100,000
- Only 7% of the conversion is tax-free. 93% is taxable.

Solution:

- Rollover pre-tax IRAs into a 401(k) (including a Solo 401(k)) before doing the backdoor Roth

Action Step: If you have other IRAs, talk to your financial advisor or CPA before doing a backdoor Roth. You may need to consolidate or transfer accounts first.

Who Should Consider a Backdoor Roth IRA?

Great fit if you:

- Are over the income limit for regular Roth IRA contributions
- Have little to no pre-tax IRA balances (or can move them)
- Want tax-free income in retirement
- Plan to leave tax-free assets to heirs

May not be worth it if:

- You have large existing pre-tax IRAs you can't transfer
- You don't want to deal with the extra forms
- Your income is inconsistent and varies below/above limits

Action Step: Run a pro-rata test: total non-deductible contributions divided by total IRA balances = tax-free portion.

Why Roth Accounts Matter for Dentists

You already face a high tax burden. You'll likely have taxable income in retirement (from 401(k)s, Social Security, practice sale, etc.)

Roth accounts offer:

- Tax diversification
- No required minimum distributions (RMDs)
- Flexibility for big purchases in retirement
- Legacy planning advantages

Roth dollars are the most flexible dollars you can have later in life.

Dentist Scenarios: Backdoor Roth in Real Life

Dr. Kim: Single, 36, earns $245K/year, no traditional IRA balances.

- Contributes $7,000 to a traditional IRA
- Converts to Roth IRA the next day
- No tax owed
- Files Form 8606 with her return

Drs. James & Monica: Married, own a practice, earn $510K combined.

- Already have 401(k)s and defined benefit plan
- Use backdoor Roths annually for both spouses to build tax-free retirement layer

Dr. Patel: 50, had $150K in a rollover IRA from a prior job.

- Learns about the pro-rata rule and rolls that IRA into his Solo 401(k) before doing the backdoor Roth

Mistakes to Avoid

- Forgetting to file Form 8606 (IRS doesn't remind you!)
- Doing the conversion too late, causing taxable growth
- Having pre-tax IRA balances that trigger the pro-rata rule
- Confusing Roth IRA *contributions* with *conversions*

Action Step: Before you start, print and read IRS Form 8606. Familiarize yourself with what you're signing up for.

Tips for Staying Organized

- Keep Roth and Traditional IRA accounts separate
- Name the backdoor conversion transactions clearly (e.g., "2025 Roth Conversion")
- Track each year's Form 8606s—store with your tax returns
- Set a calendar reminder every January to repeat the strategy

Working With Professionals

You'll want:

- A tax-savvy financial advisor
- A CPA who understands pro-rata and Form 8606

This strategy isn't hard—but it is easy to mess up. A $200 mistake today could mean a $2,000 tax bill later.

Action Step: Ask your advisor: "Have you helped other dentists with backdoor Roth IRAs?" If not, find one who has.

Closing Thoughts: Little Door, Big Opportunity

It's called a backdoor. But it can open a front-row seat to long-term tax savings.

This isn't a strategy for everyone. But if you're a high-income dentist who wants to build wealth with intention, the backdoor Roth IRA is one of the most powerful tools available.

It's smart. It's simple—when done correctly. And it's something you can repeat, year after year, to build a deep reserve of tax-free wealth for your future.

Don't let complexity keep you from clarity. Ask questions. Take action. Open the door.

Because what's on the other side? Financial freedom. And that's worth the paperwork.

Part 5: The Retirement Years – Planning the Exit

Part 5 of *Financial Literacy For Dentists* brings the journey full circle—focusing on how to exit dentistry with dignity, purpose, and financial peace of mind. After decades of education, hard work, and career-building, this section helps you turn the page to a new chapter: retirement. But not just any retirement—one that's planned, personalized, and fully aligned with your values, lifestyle, and legacy goals.

We begin with a simple but essential truth: retirement is not a finish line—it's a transition. And like any successful transition, it takes intention, timing, and the right strategy. We help you answer critical questions like:

- When can I realistically retire?
- How much is enough?
- Should I sell my practice, phase out gradually, or shift into a new role?

This section explores the three phases of retirement planning: preparation, transition, and execution. You'll learn how to:

- Assess your retirement readiness through cash flow analysis and net worth tracking
- Maximize Social Security and Medicare decisions in coordination with your retirement date
- Determine how to draw down your assets strategically—so you don't

outlive your money
- Decide whether to sell your practice, pass it on, or turn it into a semi-passive income stream

We also tackle the emotional side of retirement. What happens to your identity when you no longer have patients to see or a schedule to control? What will fill your days, your heart, and your mind? Whether it's mentoring, traveling, volunteering, or launching a second act—this section supports you in reimagining life after dentistry with intention.

This part also includes:

- Tax-efficient withdrawal strategies from IRAs, 401(k)s, and brokerage accounts
- Long-term care planning and insurance options for later-life health needs
- Estate planning updates and charitable giving frameworks
- Protecting your surviving spouse or heirs through proper beneficiary designations and legacy planning

By the end of Part 5, you'll feel equipped to retire *to* something, not just *from* something. You'll have a roadmap that blends financial freedom with personal fulfillment, ensuring that your exit from dentistry is not the end—but a launchpad into a meaningful, well-designed life chapter that honors everything you've worked for.

Chapter 42: Should a Dentist Invest in Real Estate or Restaurants?

Let's start with the question no one asks out loud:

"Am I getting into this because it's smart—or because it *sounds* successful?"

Real estate and restaurants are two of the most talked-about investments among dentists.

You hear the stories. You see the headlines. You meet a colleague who bought a strip mall or invested in a new tapas place downtown and suddenly you're wondering...

Should I be doing that too?

This chapter is here to help you think clearly and critically about these two high-risk, high-reward paths—so you can make a decision that fits your actual life, not your ego.

Let's compare, contrast, and dig deep.

Real Estate: The Classic Wealth Builder

Real estate has long been considered one of the most consistent ways to build long-term wealth.

Types of real estate investment:

- Single-family rental homes
- Multi-family apartments
- Commercial buildings (retail, office, industrial)
- Triple-net leases

- Syndications (group real estate investments)
- REITs (public or private)

Why dentists are drawn to real estate:

- Tangible assets (you can touch it)
- Perceived control
- Leverage (banks help you buy more than you could with cash alone)
- Tax advantages (depreciation, cost segregation, 1031 exchanges)

The appeal: "Mailbox money." Passive income that supplements your dental practice earnings.

Pros:

- Appreciation potential
- Rental income stream
- Tax benefits
- Can be passed down generationally

Cons:

- Requires time and management (or hiring someone who does)
- Upfront costs can be high (20–30% down + closing + repairs)
- Not always liquid (can't sell overnight like stocks)
- Tenants, toilets, turnover

Real-world scenario: Dr. Kim purchased a duplex and outsourced property management. After 3 years, the property appreciated 20%, cash flowed $400/month, and she refinanced to pull equity for a second property.

Action Step: If considering real estate, decide first: Active or passive? Are you hands-on or looking for a syndication or REIT?

Restaurants: Risk, Romance, and Return?

Here's the brutal truth:

Restaurants are one of the highest-risk investments in any industry.

Failure rate:

- Nearly 60% fail within 3 years
- Thin margins
- High overhead and labor costs
- Requires operations expertise (that most dentists don't have)

Why dentists still consider it:

- Emotional attachment ("I love food")
- Legacy or family interests
- Glamour and social status ("I own a cool place")
- Belief in the entrepreneur running it

Pros:

- If it works, cash flow can be strong
- Status and community involvement
- Investment of passion

Cons:

- High failure rate
- Industry complexity
- Burnout is common
- Limited resale value

Real-world scenario: Dr. Lopez invested $100K into his cousin's upscale burger concept. It opened, made waves... then closed in 18 months due to staffing shortages and location issues. The investment was lost.

Action Step: Before investing in a restaurant, request the business plan, pro forma, and clear exit strategy. Be brutally honest: is this logic or loyalty?

Comparing the Two

Risk Level:

- Real estate = Moderate (with good location and management)
- Restaurants = High

Control:

- Real estate = More control, especially if you own the property
- Restaurants = Less control unless you're running it day-to-day

Liquidity:

- Real estate = Illiquid, but has equity options
- Restaurants = Very illiquid, often no buyers for failed ventures

Tax Benefits:

- Real estate = Excellent
- Restaurants = Limited unless you materially participate

Learning Curve:

- Real estate = Steep at first, flattens over time
- Restaurants = Always steep if you're not in the industry

Time Commitment:

- Real estate = Variable
- Restaurants = Constant, even for investors

Legacy Potential:

- Real estate = Can create generational wealth
- Restaurants = Usually not built for inheritance

Action Step: Write out what you want from the investment: cash flow? legacy? involvement? tax benefits? Then match the vehicle to the vision.

Alternatives That Blend Both Worlds

1. Own the real estate, lease to a restaurant:

- You earn rent
- They run the restaurant
- You benefit from appreciation

2. Invest in a franchise instead of a startup:

- Proven systems
- Better support
- Higher initial investment but less risk

3. Buy a dental office building and lease it to yourself:

- Tax deduction for rent
- Wealth building through equity

Action Step: Don't say yes to any deal that doesn't have audited financials, a written business plan, and a professional management team.

Common Mistakes to Avoid

- Investing with emotion, not analysis
- Partnering without a formal agreement
- No understanding of industry benchmarks
- Not protecting your personal assets (LLCs matter!)
- No plan for how to exit

Action Step: If someone pitches you an investment, ask: "What's the worst-case scenario—and am I truly okay with that?"

Closing Thoughts: You Don't Have to Say Yes to Every Opportunity

Just because you're a dentist with extra income doesn't mean you need to become a part-time landlord or restaurateur.

Every investment has a risk-return tradeoff. Real estate has a track record. Restaurants have sizzle—but usually not steak.

Know your role. Know your limits. Know your goals.

You've worked hard to build wealth in dentistry. Make sure your investments work just as hard *for you.*

Say yes to what aligns—not what just sounds impressive at a dinner party.

Because your money should serve your life—not the other way around.

Chapter 43: Investing in Land – Is It Worth It?

Land.

It's the oldest asset class in history. It's finite, tangible, and in theory—indestructible.

But is it a good investment for dentists?

You've likely heard someone say, "Buy land. They're not making any more of it." And while that statement is technically true, it doesn't mean every land deal is golden.

This chapter is about cutting through the myth, the mystery, and the marketing. We're going to explore whether investing in raw land is a smart move—or just a seductive story.

Like all chapters in this book, our goal is clarity. So let's walk through land investing step-by-step, with real talk, real examples, and tools to help you decide if this path is right for you.

What Exactly Is "Land Investing"?

Investing in land generally means buying property that:

- Has no building or development on it ("raw land")
- Is purchased with the intention of appreciation, resale, or development
- Often requires patience (and a plan)

Types of land investments:

- Rural acreage
- Infill lots (within city limits)
- Agricultural land
- Timberland
- Recreational/hunting land
- Land for future commercial or residential development

Action Step: Ask yourself: Are you interested in land for growth, use, or legacy?

Why Dentists Consider Land Investments

1. **Tangible and easy to understand** You can see it. Walk it. Fence it. It's not like Bitcoin or biotech stocks.
2. **Long-term growth potential** In fast-growing regions, raw land can appreciate dramatically.
3. **Low holding costs (sometimes)** No structures means no tenants or maintenance—just property taxes and maybe minimal upkeep.
4. **Diversification** Land doesn't move like the stock market. It provides an alternative store of value.
5. **Legacy or lifestyle** Some dentists buy land to one day build a home, a retreat, or pass it down to their kids.

Action Step: Write out your reason for wanting land. Is it financial, emotional, or a mix?

The Pros of Land Investing

Appreciation potential Especially if you buy near the path of development (think highways, suburbs, commercial corridors).

Low management No 2 a.m. tenant calls. No roof leaks. Just open space.

Leverage Some banks will finance land with 25–50% down.

Creative use cases Rent it to farmers. Lease it to cell towers. Use it for outdoor events or storage.

Tax benefits (in some cases) If used agriculturally or as part of a conservation easement, you may receive tax breaks.

Real-world example: Dr. Sam bought 10 acres outside a booming Texas town in 2017. A developer offered 3x his purchase price in 2022. He sold, rolled profits into another property via a 1031 exchange.

The Cons of Land Investing

No cash flow Most land does not produce income unless rented for farming or other uses.

Liquidity challenges It can take months—or years—to sell land, especially in a downturn.

Property taxes Even if unused, land still accrues taxes annually.

Zoning and legal limitations What you *think* you can do with land and what's *legally allowed* are often different.

Market risk Buy in the wrong area or at the wrong time, and you could hold an underperforming asset indefinitely.

Action Step: Before you buy, research: zoning, utilities access, floodplains, future road maps, and recent comparable land sales.

How to Evaluate a Land Deal

1. **Location, location, location** Growth trends, nearby development, infrastructure expansion
2. **Access and usability** Can you drive up to it? Is it buildable? Is it flat or wooded?
3. **Utilities** Is there electricity? Sewer? Water? If not, how much to install?
4. **Zoning and permitted uses** Can it be used for residential, commercial, or agriculture?
5. **Environmental restrictions** Check wetlands, endangered species, or historical protections
6. **Price per acre compared to comps** Don't overpay because of emotion or optimism
7. **Exit strategy** How will you profit: resale, lease, or development?

Action Step: Before making an offer, call the county planning office. Ask what's allowed and what's planned nearby.

Financing Land

Options include:

- Cash (often gets discounts)
- Local banks or credit unions (especially rural)
- Seller financing (common in land deals)
- Self-directed IRAs (for retirement investing)

Challenges:

- Higher down payments (often 25–50%)
- Shorter loan terms
- Higher interest rates
- May require balloon payments

Action Step: Talk to 2–3 lenders before assuming you'll use financing. Land lending is very different than home mortgages.

Land Scams and Red Flags

Common traps:

- Overpriced "vacation parcels" marketed to out-of-state buyers
- No road access or utility infrastructure
- Sellers who won't provide a clear title
- Flood-prone or unusable plots

Red flags:

- "Too good to be true" pricing
- High-pressure sales tactics
- Lack of comps in the area

Action Step: Always get a title report. Always walk the land. Never buy sight unseen.

Who Should *Not* Invest in Land

- Dentists with no emergency fund or liquid savings
- Anyone looking for short-term cash flow
- Buyers who hate uncertainty or long timelines
- People who haven't run the numbers

Action Step: Ask yourself: Can I hold this for 10+ years with no income and no stress?

Alternative Land Strategies

1. **Partnering with developers** Buy and hold until rezoning, then sell at a profit
2. **Leasing land** To solar companies, farmers, event companies
3. **Conservation or donation** For tax advantages and charitable giving
4. **Buy land, build tiny homes or cabins** And rent them short-term

Real-world example: Dr. Renee bought a wooded lot, cleared space for three luxury tents, and now earns $3,000/month via a glamping platform.

Closing Thoughts: Dirt Can Build Dreams—If You Buy It Wisely

Land is not a magic bullet. It won't save a shaky financial plan. But it *can* be a powerful part of your wealth-building strategy—if done thoughtfully.

Buy with logic, not lust. Use patience, not pressure. And never invest just because "someone you know" made money doing it.

Your path is your own. Your goals are your compass.

If land fits? Great. If not? That's wisdom, too.

Because financial success as a dentist doesn't require a ranch or rural plot. Just vision, values, and a strategy you can stand on—literally or figuratively.

You've got this. One acre—or one action step—at a time.

Chapter 44: Taking Investment Advice from Colleagues – The Pros, Cons, and Pitfalls

Let's start with a familiar scene.

You're at a dental conference. The lecture just ended. You're sipping coffee in the hallway. Someone you trust—a dentist who seems to have it all together—mentions their latest investment.

They're making big returns. They're buying into a real estate deal. They're raving about a tech startup.

And suddenly, your retirement plan, your 401(k), your carefully selected mutual funds… they feel boring.

So what do you do?

This chapter is about one of the most powerful forces in dentistry that no one talks about:

Peer influence.

Especially when it comes to money.

We're going to unpack when to listen, when to smile politely, and when to step back and do your own due diligence. Because while colleagues can be a wealth of knowledge—they can also lead you down paths that weren't meant for you.

Why Dentists Rely on Each Other for Financial Advice

1. **Shared experience** You trust your peers because they get your world—student debt, burnout, overhead, production goals.

2. **Similar income levels** It feels easier to relate to someone earning what you earn.
3. **Fear of missing out (FOMO)** No one wants to be the dentist who *didn't* invest early in the "next big thing."
4. **Lack of formal education** Most dental programs don't teach personal finance, so dentists turn to each other.

Action Step: Write down where you currently get most of your investment ideas. Is it a podcast, a peer, a planner, or a mix?

The Pros of Peer-Based Financial Advice

1. **Real-world examples** Peers speak from lived experience, not theory.
2. **Access to niche opportunities** Some of the best private deals are passed through word-of-mouth in dental circles.
3. **Accountability and motivation** If your colleague is investing, saving, and planning—it might inspire you to do the same.
4. **Learning curve shortcut** They've already made mistakes. You can learn from them.

Real-World Scenario: Dr. Patel joined a dental-specific real estate syndication because two trusted colleagues had been with the group for years. He vetted it himself, but their experience gave him confidence.

The Cons and Cautions

1. **No two financial lives are the same** Your tax situation, goals, risk tolerance, and liquidity needs may be totally different—even if your incomes are similar.
2. **Survivorship bias** People rarely talk about the deals they *lost* money on.
3. **Hidden incentives** Some colleagues may get referral fees for recommending investment opportunities.
4. **Lack of financial training** Being great at clinical dentistry doesn't mean someone understands investment risk, diversification, or tax

strategy.

Real-World Scenario: Dr. Lisa invested $50,000 into a private dental tech startup after hearing about it from a friend. It failed. She later learned her colleague received a 5% referral bonus.

Action Step: Ask yourself: Would I make this decision if no one else I knew was doing it?

How to Vet Peer-Recommended Investments

1. **Do your own due diligence** Request full documentation. Read it. Ask questions.
2. **Understand the business model** How does it make money? How do you get paid?
3. **Check for third-party validation** Is there an independent CPA or legal team reviewing the deal?
4. **Assess risk vs. your overall plan** Does this fit your timeline, liquidity needs, and portfolio strategy?
5. **Confirm if your peer has a financial interest** Don't be afraid to ask: "Are you being compensated for referring me?"

Action Step: Build a checklist for any investment over $10,000. Include questions about liquidity, taxes, fees, and exit strategies.

When Listening to Peers Makes Sense

- You're early in your journey and want relatable models
- The peer has a proven track record *and* a clear understanding of the deal
- You're still going to run it past your financial planner or CPA

When It Doesn't

- You feel pressure or urgency to decide
- You don't fully understand the investment

- The only reason you're considering it is because someone else is doing it
- You're in a financially fragile place (debt-heavy, under-saved, low liquidity)

What to Say When You Want to Say "No"

Sometimes, the hardest part is turning down a peer's recommendation. Try:

- "Thanks for thinking of me. I'm keeping things simple this year."
- "I really appreciate it, but I'm sticking to my written plan."
- "Sounds great—just not aligned with my risk tolerance right now."

You're not rejecting them. You're protecting your future.

Creating a Trusted Financial Inner Circle

You need more than peer suggestions. You need a team.

Ideal financial circle includes:

- A fee-based financial advisor (fiduciary)
- A dental-savvy CPA
- A business attorney (if you're investing in entities)
- A mentor who's done what you want to do

Action Step: List your current financial team. Where are the gaps?

Real Talk: Peer Pressure Isn't Just for Teenagers

It's real in financial circles too. And it's especially real in professions like dentistry, where success is visible—and often tied to lifestyle.

But the car they drive, the lake house they built, or the story they told at lunch? That's not your benchmark.

Your plan is. Your goals are.

And the more you anchor yourself to *your* version of success, the less swayed you'll be by someone else's.

Closing Thoughts: Learn From Others, Decide For Yourself

Your colleagues can inspire you. Your peers can educate you. But only you are responsible for your financial decisions.

Make them with clarity. Make them with intention. Make them with people who help you think, not just spend.

Because wealth isn't built by imitation. It's built by alignment.

And when you get that part right? Everything else falls into place.

You've got this.

Chapter 45: Paying Off Student Loans – When, How, and Why

Let's get honest: student loans are a shadow that follows many dentists long after graduation.

They're heavy. They're stressful. And they often come with a side of shame, confusion, or frustration.

You've probably asked yourself:

- Should I pay them off as fast as possible?
- Should I invest instead?
- Is refinancing a smart move—or a trap?
- What about forgiveness programs?

This chapter isn't here to guilt you. It's here to *guide* you.

Whether you owe $200,000 or $800,000, there's a path forward. One that balances your financial goals, your emotional peace, and your long-term vision.

Let's unpack the real questions: When should you pay off your loans? How should you do it? And most importantly—*why* are you choosing the strategy that you are?

Understanding Dental School Debt

Average dental school debt in 2025: ~$305,000 (private schools often exceed $400,000)

Common types of loans:

- Federal Direct Loans (subsidized and unsubsidized)
- Graduate PLUS Loans
- Private loans
- Institutional or school-based loans

Loan features to understand:

- Interest rate
- Grace period
- Capitalization rules
- Repayment term
- Federal vs. private loan protections

Action Step: Make a spreadsheet or use a loan aggregator (like studentaid.gov) to list:

- Loan type
- Balance
- Interest rate
- Monthly payment
- Servicer

You can't build a strategy until you know what you're working with.

The Three Main Strategies

1. Aggressive Payoff

- Goal: Pay off all student loans in 3–7 years
- Ideal for: High earners, low living expenses, practice owners, debt-averse dentists

Pros:

- Peace of mind

- More money freed up for future investing
- Total interest paid is lower

Cons:

- Missed opportunity to invest in higher-return vehicles
- Potential burnout if lifestyle is overly restricted

2. Income-Driven Repayment (IDR) + Forgiveness

- Goal: Make minimum payments for 20–25 years, then receive forgiveness (PSLF or IDR forgiveness)
- Ideal for: Associates, academic dentists, public service roles, those with very high debt-to-income ratio

Pros:

- Cash flow flexibility
- Potential for forgiveness
- PSLF forgiveness is tax-free

Cons:

- Long timeline
- IDR forgiveness may be taxable
- Balance may grow before forgiveness kicks in

3. Refinance and Pay Strategically

- Goal: Reduce interest rate and set a custom payoff timeline
- Ideal for: Private loan holders, federal loan borrowers not pursuing forgiveness

Pros:

- Lower interest = less paid over time
- Flexible repayment terms (5–20 years)

Cons:

- Loss of federal protections (deferment, IDR, PSLF)
- Variable rates may rise

Real-World Scenarios

Dr. Kim (Private Practice Owner)

- Owes $250,000, earning $220,000/year
- Refinanced to 3.75% fixed for 10 years
- Aggressively pays $4,000/month and will be debt-free in 6 years

Dr. Lopez (Academic Faculty)

- Owes $480,000, earning $120,000/year
- On PAYE, pursuing PSLF after 10 years of nonprofit employment
- Projected forgiveness: $320,000

Dr. Patel (Startup Owner)

- Owes $310,000, earning $150,000 (but reinvesting in his practice)
- On SAVE plan for cash flow flexibility, plans to refinance in 2 years

Action Step: Map your personal scenario. What's your income? Loan type? Career path? Comfort with debt?

Should You Invest or Pay Off Loans?

This is the big question. And there's no one-size-fits-all answer.

Consider:

- Your interest rate vs. expected investment returns
- Your emotional tolerance for debt
- Your financial goals (home buying, practice ownership, family planning)

General rule of thumb: If your loan rate is above 6.5%, prioritize payoff. If it's below 4.5%, consider investing instead (especially in retirement accounts).

Action Step: Run the math: compare total interest saved vs. projected investment growth (with your advisor or tools like NerdWallet's calculators).

Understanding Forgiveness Options

Public Service Loan Forgiveness (PSLF):

- 10 years of qualifying payments
- Must work for qualifying nonprofit or government employer
- Tax-free forgiveness

IDR Forgiveness (SAVE, PAYE, IBR):

- 20–25 years of payments
- Any remaining balance forgiven
- May be taxable (pending IRS rules and future laws)

Important: You must recertify income annually. Track every payment.

Action Step: If pursuing PSLF, file the PSLF Employment Certification Form *every year.*

To Refinance or Not to Refinance?

Refinancing makes sense if:

- You have private loans with high interest
- You're not using federal loan forgiveness or deferment programs
- You want to save interest and customize your payoff timeline

Top lenders (2025):

- Laurel Road
- SoFi
- Earnest
- Credible (comparison tool)

Caution: Refinancing is *permanent.* Once you leave federal loans, there's no going back.

Action Step: Get quotes from 3–5 lenders. Look for fixed rates, no origination fees, and borrower protections (some offer deferment options).

Mental Health and Student Loan Stress

This part matters. Because dental school debt isn't just numbers. It's emotional. It's heavy. It can cause guilt, fear, and even avoidance.

Strategies to stay mentally grounded:

- Don't ignore it—organize it
- Celebrate small milestones ("Paid off $50K!")
- Share your plan with a financial coach or advisor
- Join a student loan accountability group (yes, they exist!)

Reflection: You are not your loan balance. You are not a failure because you have debt. You are a high-earning, highly trained professional with options.

Tools and Resources for Dentists

- **StudentAid.gov** – View federal loan details and servicers
- **VIN Foundation** – Free loan repayment simulator for veterinarians and dentists
- **White Coat Investor / Student Loan Planner** – Financial education for professionals
- **Certified Student Loan Professionals (CSLPs)** – Advisors with specialized training

Action Step: Schedule a student loan strategy session—even if you think you know what you're doing. Confirmation is clarity.

Closing Thoughts: Your Debt Does Not Define You

Dentistry is a career of delayed gratification. And for many, student loans are the heaviest weight they carry into their financial future.

But debt is not a death sentence. It's a puzzle. And every puzzle has a solution.

You can build wealth *while* managing debt. You can own a practice, buy a home, and retire with peace.

The key is to stop ignoring the balance and start owning the strategy.

You've already done the hard part: becoming a dentist. Now it's time to let smart planning transform that degree into the wealth—and life—you deserve.

Chapter 46: Understanding the Economy, Markets, and the Media Noise

If you've ever found yourself glued to CNBC, scrolling through headlines, or texting your financial advisor with, "Should I be worried?"—this chapter is for you.

As a dentist, your days are filled with clinical decisions, patient care, and practice operations. But when it comes to the economy, the stock market, and financial headlines, it's easy to feel like you've missed a class everyone else took.

Here's the truth: You didn't miss anything. You just haven't had it explained in a way that makes sense for your world.

This chapter breaks it all down—from inflation to interest rates, market corrections to media panic—in a clear, calm way. We'll also show you how to stay grounded when the news cycle tries to throw you off balance.

The Economy vs. The Market: What's the Difference?

Let's start with this: The economy is *not* the same thing as the stock market.

The economy is the big picture. It includes jobs, GDP, consumer spending, inflation, interest rates, housing, and more.

The stock market is a forward-looking system of investors reacting to what they *expect* will happen.

Key difference:

- The economy tells you how things *are*

- The stock market reflects what people *think will happen next*

That's why the market can rise during a recession—or fall during a boom.

Action Step: Start tracking what headlines are talking about. Are they discussing the economy or the stock market? It's rarely both.

What Drives the Economy (And Why You Should Care)

1. **Consumer spending** Dentists are in a consumer-based business. When people feel good about their finances, they invest in their smiles.
2. **Employment** Job security fuels spending. High unemployment usually means cautious patients.
3. **Inflation** Rising prices affect everything—from your supplies to your staff salaries to what patients are willing to pay.
4. **Interest rates** These impact everything from your practice loans to your mortgage.
5. **Government policy** Taxes, healthcare subsidies, student loan rules—all can impact your bottom line.

What Moves the Market?

The market is not a reflection of today. It's a prediction engine.

What influences it:

- Corporate earnings
- Interest rate changes
- Fed announcements
- Geopolitical tension
- Investor sentiment

Short-term market moves = emotion Long-term market growth = business fundamentals

Action Step: If you're investing for retirement, focus on the long-term trend—not this week's headlines.

Common Terms Made Simple

Recession: Two quarters of declining GDP (often accompanied by job loss, lower spending)

Inflation: Prices rising across the economy (measured by CPI)

Deflation: Prices falling—can be just as scary as inflation

Interest Rates: The cost of borrowing money—set largely by the Federal Reserve

The Fed: America's central bank, which uses interest rates to control inflation and stimulate growth

Bear Market: A drop of 20% or more from recent market highs

Bull Market: A rising market—typically fueled by strong fundamentals or optimism

Correction: A short-term drop of 10–20%—common and usually healthy

The Role of the Media (and Why It Makes You Anxious)

Media runs on attention. And fear is the fastest way to get attention.

You rarely hear:

- "Markets fell 4%—a normal correction." You hear:
- "MARKET MELTDOWN! IS YOUR RETIREMENT SAFE?"

Why this matters: Emotional headlines can cause emotional decisions. And emotional investing is almost always bad investing.

Action Step: Limit financial news exposure. Check your long-term plan quarterly—not hourly.

How This Affects Dentists Specifically

1. **Practice loans:** Higher interest rates = higher costs to buy or expand your practice
2. **Patient behavior:** Economic uncertainty = more cancellations, delayed treatments, focus on essential vs. elective
3. **Staff wages:** Inflation and employment trends impact what you must offer to attract and retain staff
4. **Retirement planning:** Down markets can spook you—especially if

you're close to retirement

The Power of Staying Invested

Let's say you panicked during a downturn and pulled out of the market.
Here's what could happen:

- You miss the 10 best days of recovery
- Your long-term returns are significantly lower

Example: Dr. Lopez left the market in March 2020 during COVID. Missed April's rebound. Lost $75,000 in missed growth.

Action Step: Create an investment policy statement (IPS) that outlines your plan—and stick to it.

What You Can Actually Control

You can't control inflation. You can't control the market. But you can control:

- Your savings rate
- Your investment allocation
- Your spending habits
- Your response to media

Action Step: Focus your energy on the "controllables." That's where peace lives.

Tools to Stay Grounded

- A fee-only advisor who isn't trying to sell you fear or products
- A written financial plan
- Automatic contributions to retirement accounts
- Yearly check-ins—not daily panic sessions

Final Thoughts: Filters Over Frenzy

The world is loud. Especially the financial world.

But you don't have to absorb all that noise. You can build filters:

- Is this headline designed to inform me—or scare me?
- Does this change my long-term goals?
- Would I feel the same way if I turned off the TV?

You're not a hedge fund. You're not a day trader. You're a dentist with a long horizon, a growing practice, and a plan.

Trust the plan. Tune out the panic. Keep showing up—for your patients, your practice, and your peace of mind.

Because financial confidence isn't about knowing everything. It's about knowing enough to stay grounded when others are shaking.

Chapter 47: How to Start Investing – Even If You're Late to the Game

Let's start with this: You are not behind.

You are right on time—for you.

If you're reading this chapter with a sense of guilt, panic, or regret because you haven't "started investing yet" or you feel like everyone else got a head start, take a breath.

This chapter is for you. Whether you're 35, 45, or 55. Whether you're just getting your finances under control or finally feeling ready to put money to work.

You're not too late. And your future is still bright.

Let's build your investment game plan from the ground up—with clarity, compassion, and confidence.

Why Dentists Sometimes Delay Investing

1. **Student debt:** You spent years paying off (or managing) six figures of loans.
2. **Practice ownership:** Starting or buying a dental practice eats up capital and focus.
3. **Lifestyle inflation:** Income rises. So do expectations, family needs, and expenses.
4. **Overwhelm:** The investing world feels complex, risky, or full of jargon.
5. **Shame or comparison:** You see peers talking about Roth IRAs or

passive income and feel like you've missed your shot.

Here's the truth: you haven't.

The only bad investment strategy is doing nothing out of fear or perfectionism.

The Three Pillars of Catch-Up Investing

1. Clarity: Know what you have, what you owe, and what you need. **2. Consistency:** Automate your investing and treat it like a monthly bill. **3. Compounding:** Give your money enough time and space to grow.

Action Step: Run a simple net worth snapshot:

- Assets: savings, real estate, retirement accounts
- Liabilities: mortgage, student loans, credit card debt
- Net Worth = Assets - Liabilities

Start Where You Are (Even If It's $200/Month)

It's not about how much you invest. It's about *starting.*

Even $200/month, consistently invested over 15–20 years, can grow into six figures.

Where to start investing:

- Roth IRA (if eligible)
- Traditional IRA or SEP IRA (if self-employed)
- 401(k) or Solo 401(k)
- Brokerage account (for after-tax investing)

Action Step: Set up auto-drafts. Treat your investments like rent: non-negotiable.

Understand the Basics (Without Getting a Finance Degree)

Stocks = ownership in companies Bonds = loans to companies/government Mutual Funds = baskets of stocks or bonds Index Funds = low-cost funds that track a market index ETFs = like index funds, but trade like stocks

Action Step: Pick 1-2 index funds to start. (Ex: S&P 500 index, total U.S. market index)

Prioritize Tax-Advantaged Accounts

Why? Less tax = more money compounding for you.

Top picks for dentists:

- Roth IRA (tax-free growth)
- SEP IRA (great for practice owners)
- Solo 401(k) (huge limits if self-employed)
- Traditional 401(k) (tax deferral at work)

2025 contribution limits:

- Roth IRA: $7,000/year (catch-up = $8,000 if age 50+)
- 401(k): $23,000/year (catch-up = $30,500 if age 50+)

Action Step: Max out Roth or 401(k) first. Then invest in a brokerage if you have more.

Overcoming the "I'm Too Late" Mindset

Time is powerful, but it's not everything. Contribution size and consistency matter too.

Example: Dr. Garcia started investing at age 45. Saved $3,000/month into a 401(k). With 20 years of moderate returns (7%), she'll have $1.5M+ by retirement.

Action Step: Focus on the next 10 years—not the last 10.

What to Avoid When You're Starting Late

1. **Chasing high-risk investments** You don't need crypto moonshots. You need stability and compounding.
2. **Listening to random influencers** Get advice from fiduciaries, not TikTok.
3. **Analysis paralysis** You don't need the "perfect" fund to start. You just need to start.

4. **Trying to "make up" for lost time with debt** Don't borrow to invest. Ever.

How to Build a Portfolio in Your 40s, 50s, or 60s

1. Diversify. Don't bet on one company or one fund. **2. Lower fees.** Index funds beat most active funds long-term. **3. Adjust for risk.** Be more conservative as you near retirement.

Sample Allocation (age 45):

- 70% stocks (U.S. + international)
- 25% bonds
- 5% cash or real estate

Action Step: Use a target-date fund (e.g., Vanguard 2045) if you want simplicity.

Should You Work Longer? Maybe.

Working just 3–5 years longer can massively increase your retirement confidence.

Why it helps:

- More time to invest
- Delayed withdrawals
- More Social Security (if you wait past 62)
- Lower sequence-of-return risk

Action Step: Run a retirement projection with a financial planner. Test different retirement ages.

Real-World Dentist Scenarios

Dr. Nina (Age 48):

- Never invested
- Opened a Roth IRA + Solo 401(k)
- Saved $50K in 3 years with index funds

- Started feeling *excited* about her financial future

Dr. Omar (Age 55):

- Sold his practice, no retirement savings
- Invested proceeds in a 60/40 portfolio
- Delayed retirement until 68
- Projected to have $900K by then

What About the Market Being "Too High"?

Here's the secret: the market *always* feels expensive in hindsight.

The key is *time in* the market—not timing the market.

Action Step: Start a dollar-cost averaging plan. Invest monthly regardless of headlines.

Mindset Reset: You Are Not Too Late

Let go of comparison. Let go of regret. Let go of the myth that you missed your window.

You didn't.

You're still here. You're still earning. You're still learning.

And now you're doing the one thing that matters most: You're starting.

Ten years from now, your future self will thank you. Not because you got rich overnight. But because you chose to stop standing still.

Closing Thoughts: You've Still Got Time—and Power

Dentists are some of the highest-earning professionals in the country.

That means you can save more, catch up faster, and build real wealth—even if you didn't start in your 20s.

It's not about when you start. It's about *starting now.*

With clarity. With consistency. And with the quiet confidence that comes from choosing progress over perfection.

Chapter 48: Helping Without Hurting – Financial Support for Loved Ones

There's a deep, personal satisfaction in being able to help the people you love.

Whether it's aging parents, a struggling sibling, or your own children—you worked hard, built a career, and now you're in a position to offer support. That's something to be proud of.

But here's the challenge:

How do you support others financially *without* damaging your own financial future? How do you give generously *without* enabling dependency or creating silent resentment?

This chapter isn't about telling you who to help or how much. It's about helping you do it with intention, boundaries, and balance.

You don't have to choose between compassion and financial wisdom. You can practice both.

The Emotional Pressure of Being the "Successful One"

Dentists often become the financial anchor in their extended families. You make a good income. You drive a nice car. You own your practice.

But what people *don't* see is:

- The student debt you carried for a decade
- The staff raises you're juggling
- The retirement savings you're trying to catch up on

Action Step: Write down your current obligations (mortgage, staff payroll, kids' education, savings goals). Visualizing your financial landscape helps you give from a grounded place—not guilt.

Who You Might Be Supporting

1. Elderly parents

- Assisted living, medical bills, in-home care

2. Siblings or extended family

- Temporary help, housing support, legal aid

3. Adult children

- College tuition, living expenses, car payments

4. Grandchildren

- Education funding, trust accounts

5. Friends or close community members

- One-time emergencies, loans, business investments

Support looks different in every family. What matters is that it aligns with *your* values and goals.

The Hidden Costs of Financial Support

Helping someone out can feel good in the moment. But long-term, it can:

- Drain your retirement savings
- Delay your own debt payoff
- Shift financial boundaries in ways that are hard to reset

- Create dependency instead of empowerment

Real-World Scenario: Dr. Ramos supported her brother during his divorce. She paid his rent for a year. Five years later, he still asks for help. She's now 54 and behind on retirement.

Action Step: Before you give, ask: "Am I solving a problem—or postponing it?"

Setting Boundaries Without Guilt

Boundaries are a form of love. They say: I care about you *and* I care about me.

How to set boundaries:

- Set a dollar limit per year for family support
- Offer one-time help, not ongoing open-ended aid
- Have "support scripts" ready for tough conversations

Examples:

- "I can't pay your rent, but I can help you apply for assistance."
- "We've decided not to co-sign loans—but we're happy to review your budget together."

Action Step: Write 2-3 supportive but clear phrases you can use when asked for money.

The Pros and Cons of Gifting vs. Lending

Gifting: Pros: Clean, no resentment, generosity Cons: Expectations, less control, may impact other goals

Lending: Pros: Teaches accountability, can preserve boundaries Cons: Strains relationships if unpaid, tracking/logistics

Golden Rule: Never lend more than you're willing to lose.

Formalizing Support: When to Put It in Writing

If you're giving large sums:

- Use gift letters (for mortgage down payments)
- Consider promissory notes (for loans)
- Involve an estate planning attorney (for long-term support)

This protects both parties and keeps things clear.

Action Step: For any financial gift over $10,000, put it in writing—even if it's to family.

What About Supporting Kids?

You want your kids to have a good life. But that doesn't mean footing the bill for everything.

Common support traps:

- Paying for adult children's lifestyles (rent, cars, luxury expenses)
- Failing to teach budgeting, credit, or job skills
- Giving too much too soon (inheritance, business ownership)

Better strategies:

- Fund a 529 plan for education
- Match their savings contributions
- Hire them in your practice with purpose

Action Step: Teach your kids to budget using their own money before college. It builds confidence and respect.

Don't Neglect Your Own Future

Supporting others should never come at the cost of:

- Skipping your retirement savings
- Not paying down your own debt
- Delaying estate planning

Visual: You can't pour from an empty cup. Secure your own oxygen mask first.

How to Say "No" Without Saying "No"

- "Let me think about how I can help."
- "We're focusing on our financial plan right now."
- "That's not in the budget this year, but I'm cheering for you."

Empathy + Clarity = Respectful Boundaries

When Generosity Turns Into Enabling

Helping is generous. But enabling is dangerous.

Warning signs:

- Repeated requests with no change in behavior
- Feeling anxious, guilty, or resentful
- Others expecting you to fix every financial issue

Reframe support: Instead of "rescuing," ask:

- "What would a sustainable solution look like?"
- "How can I support you learning, not just surviving?"

Using Financial Advisors to Facilitate Conversations

Sometimes, it helps to have a third party. A financial advisor can:

- Help you budget for support
- Model scenarios for retirement if you give XYZ amount
- Serve as a buffer in family meetings

Action Step: If you're planning to give substantial support, loop in your advisor early.

Teaching Family to Fish (Not Just Giving Them the Fish)

Empower loved ones with:

- Budgeting help

- Financial literacy books or courses
- Guidance on credit, banking, and investing
- Introductions to professionals

Generosity is best paired with education.

Legacy Giving That Doesn't Derail Your Plan

If you want to leave a legacy:

- Consider life insurance for estate equalization
- Use donor-advised funds or trusts
- Gift appreciated assets instead of cash
- Create a giving plan that's sustainable

Action Step: Build giving into your estate plan—with intention and structure.

Closing Thoughts: Boundaries Are Kindness

Helping loved ones financially can be one of the most meaningful things you do.

But only if it's done from a place of strength, not sacrifice.

Your financial life matters too. Your peace of mind is just as important.

Lead with heart. Give with intention. Support with wisdom.

That's how you help—without hurting.

Chapter 49: Stupid Investments – What to Avoid

Let's start with the obvious: no one *intends* to make a stupid investment.

But here's the hard truth: smart people—educated, successful, even financially savvy professionals—fall into traps all the time.

Dentists are no exception. In fact, dentists are *prime targets* for bad investments.

Why?

- You earn a high income
- You often have little formal financial training
- You're busy running a practice and helping patients
- You're trusted in your community and used to being in control

That combination creates the perfect setup for emotional decisions, peer pressure, and misjudged opportunities.

This chapter isn't here to shame you. It's here to protect you.

We're going to break down the red flags, expose the common traps, and help you build an investing filter that keeps you safe—and wealthy.

Let's get into it.

The Dentist Investment Stereotype

There's a reason financial advisors jokingly call some bad ideas "DDS Investments." It's not because dentists are foolish. It's because they're busy professionals who trust their friends, want passive income, and are often approached by the wrong people.

You may have heard:

- "My buddy got into a real estate syndication. I'm thinking about throwing in $100K."
- "This guy from church has a franchise opportunity I can't miss."
- "I heard crypto is the future—I don't want to miss out again."

Sound familiar?

Let's slow down and unpack why these ideas can be dangerous.

The 10 Most Common "Stupid" Investments Dentists Make

1. **Private Placements You Don't Understand** If you don't fully understand how the business works, how it makes money, and what your exit looks like—you're gambling.
2. **Real Estate Syndications Without Transparency** You see "10% projected returns"—but the risk, leverage, and operator experience are unclear.
3. **Friends and Family Ventures** Helping a cousin start a restaurant or a neighbor launch a tech startup? Unless you're ready to lose that money forever, tread carefully.
4. **Franchises Without Experience** You're a dentist, not a sandwich shop operator. Unless you're going to run the day-to-day, it's an expensive distraction.
5. **High-Fee Annuities Sold by Commission-Based Agents** Some annuities are appropriate in retirement planning. Many are sold with high commissions, poor liquidity, and low transparency.
6. **Timeshares Disguised as Investments** Vacations are great. But don't confuse a liability with an asset.
7. **Penny Stocks or Day Trading Platforms** If you're trying to get rich quick, you're playing a losing game. Volatility is not strategy.
8. **Whole Life Insurance as a Retirement Plan** Insurance has a place.

But if someone is selling you a policy as an "investment account," pause.

9. **Crypto Speculation Without a Plan** Digital assets are real. But putting 20% of your net worth in the newest token? That's not investing—that's gambling.
10. **"Can't-Miss" MLMs or Passive Income Schemes** If it sounds too good to be true and there's no transparency—it usually is.

How to Recognize Red Flags

1. **Pressure to decide quickly** "This opportunity won't last. You have to get in by Friday."
2. **No clear path to liquidity** "You'll start getting checks in a few years..."
3. **You're relying on someone else's expertise** "They've done this before. They know what they're doing."
4. **There's no independent verification** "The numbers are proprietary. But trust me, it's solid."
5. **It makes you feel smart, rich, or important** "Only a few people in this circle know about it."

Real-World Scenarios

Dr. Evans: Bought into a dental supply startup that went bust in two years. Lost $75K.

Dr. Patel: Joined a real estate deal with friends. The operator mismanaged funds. Now stuck in legal limbo.

Dr. Harris: Bought three whole life policies from a colleague who said it was "better than a 401(k)." Only now realizing the fees.

How to Protect Yourself

1. **Slow down.** Never invest under pressure.
2. **Have a written investment policy.** Set guidelines for what you will—and won't—invest in.
3. **Diversify wisely.** Stick to core investments (index funds, tax-

advantaged accounts) first.

4. **Vet every opportunity.** If it's not regulated, audited, or transparent—walk away.
5. **Use your team.** Run ideas past your financial advisor, CPA, or attorney.

Smart Investing vs. Dumb Risk-Taking

Smart Investing:

- Long-term
- Transparent
- Aligned with goals
- Reasonable returns
- Tax-conscious

Dumb Risk-Taking:

- Fast money
- No track record
- Emotion-based
- Promises of 2X returns
- Confusing paperwork

A Better Framework for Evaluating Opportunities

1. **What is it?** Can you explain the investment in two sentences? 2. **Who's involved?** What's their track record? 3. **What are the risks?** What happens if it fails? 4. **How do I get out?** What's the exit strategy? 5. **What are the fees?** Who's getting paid—and how much? 6. **How does it fit into my plan?** Does this serve a purpose—or just spark FOMO?

What to Do If You've Already Made a Bad Investment

1. **Don't double down.** More money won't fix bad fundamentals. 2. **Learn the lesson.** What red flags did you miss? 3. **Talk to your advisor.** See if anything can be salvaged. 4. **Create new rules.** Protect your future

self.

The Best Investment Dentists Can Make

It's not in someone else's business. It's not in a speculative stock.

It's in:

- Your practice
- Low-cost index funds
- Tax-advantaged retirement plans
- Paying off debt
- Continuing education

These don't get headlines. But they *build wealth.*

Closing Thoughts: You Don't Have to Chase

You don't have to chase trends, secrets, or exotic investments to succeed.

Simple, boring investing—done well and consistently—is what builds lasting wealth.

The smartest dentists aren't the ones who "get in early." They're the ones who:

- Stick to a plan
- Protect their downside
- Focus on what they can control

Avoid the noise. Avoid the hype. Avoid the pitchman.

Protect your wealth. Protect your peace.

Chapter 50: Conclusion – Dentist, Heal Thy Finances

You've made it to the final chapter. And that says something powerful about you.

Most people avoid financial topics like a root canal. You didn't. You faced your numbers. You looked under the hood of your practice, your habits, and your future. You've asked hard questions. Made new plans. Thought deeper about money than many professionals ever will.

So now, as we close this book, I want to help you zoom out. Not into more spreadsheets. Not into another budgeting tool. But into *your life*—your purpose, your peace, your next chapter.

Because financial literacy isn't just about growing net worth. It's about reclaiming control. And for dentists, that control is *earned.*

Why This Book Was Really Written

If you've been reading with a highlighter, scribbling notes in the margins, or mentally committing to changes—you already know this wasn't written by some outsider with a bunch of theories.

It was written by someone who understands the dental journey:

- The stress of production goals
- The mountain of student loans
- The delicate dance of patient care and business ownership
- The guilt of success, and the fear of not doing enough with it

And most importantly: It was written for dentists who are ready to say: "I want to master this money thing. I want to do more than just earn—I want to *build*."

That's why this book exists.

What You've Learned (and What to Do With It)

You've learned:

- How to build a financial foundation
- How to budget, save, invest, and protect your assets
- The difference between good debt and bad debt
- Why estate planning, insurance, and retirement matter—sooner than you think
- How to avoid traps, set boundaries, and think generationally

You can now:

- Hire and vet a financial advisor like a pro
- Make smarter decisions inside your practice
- Talk to your spouse or partner with more confidence
- Plan for taxes, transitions, and big purchases with less stress

In short, you've built *financial awareness.* And awareness is the first step toward wealth, security, and freedom.

Where Most Dentists Get Stuck (And How to Move Past It)

1. **Overcomplicating It** Don't let perfection be the enemy of progress. You don't need to be a financial wizard. You need a plan you understand, and the courage to stick to it.
2. **Comparing to Others** Some colleagues have bigger houses. Fancier practices. Flashier cars. That's not the measure of success. *Peace of mind is.*
3. **Waiting Too Long** The best time to start was yesterday. The second-best time is right now. If you're reading this, you're ready.

4. **Delegating Without Understanding** It's okay to work with advisors. Just make sure you understand the why—not just the what.

Action Step: Revisit your goals every year. Check in quarterly. Adjust as needed. But never stop owning the plan.

Your Financial Checklist Moving Forward

Here's what a healthy financial plan for a dentist *should* include:

- Emergency fund (3–6 months of expenses)
- Defined savings goals (home, kids, retirement)
- Tax planning strategy (with your CPA)
- Investment accounts (Roth IRA, 401(k), SEP, etc.)
- Disability and life insurance (tailored to your needs)
- Estate plan (will, trust, POA, healthcare directive)
- A relationship with a *fiduciary* financial advisor
- A budget or spending tracker (that works for *you*)
- A clear debt repayment plan (if applicable)
- A documented investment policy or philosophy
- A vision of retirement (not just the money, but the *life*)

Print this. Keep it somewhere visible. It's your compass.

To the Dentist Who Feels Behind

You are not behind. You are not broken. You are not too late.

You're just now stepping into a new level of ownership. A new level of clarity. A new level of courage.

Start where you are. With what you have. And commit to learning as you go.

To the Dentist Who's Already Successful

Keep going. But don't let success blind you to risk, waste, or burnout.

Make sure your success is working *for* you:

- Is your practice profitable *and* sustainable?
- Are you building personal wealth—not just revenue?

- Is your family protected?
- Are you *living* your values, or just funding someone else's lifestyle?

You've worked hard. Now make sure your money is working just as hard.

To the Dentist Who Wants to Leave a Legacy

You can leave more than dollars. You can leave:

- Financial literacy for your children
- Integrity in how you handled money
- A practice that empowered others
- A life of generosity, peace, and purpose

Wealth isn't just what you accumulate. It's what you *pass down.*

Build that legacy on purpose.

Your Life, Your Plan, Your Terms

This book isn't about becoming someone else's version of "wealthy." It's about becoming *your own definition of free.*

Financial freedom for a dentist might look like:

- Buying back your time
- Retiring early (or working part-time for fun)
- Paying for your kids' education
- Saying yes to causes you care about
- Never again feeling stressed about money

Whatever it is for you—define it. Then plan for it.

You don't have to get it perfect. You just have to get it moving.

One Final Note: Dentist, Heal Thyself

You know how patients ignore problems until they're in pain? You know how they think brushing harder solves everything? You know how they listen better once they trust you?

That's how money works too.

The sooner you address it, the less painful it gets. The gentler your habits, the better your long-term health. And the more trust you have—in yourself and your plan—the more peace you'll feel.

So if you remember nothing else from this book, remember this:

You are not just a dentist. You are the CEO of your financial life. You are capable of making smart, confident, intentional money decisions. You are allowed to dream. You are allowed to be wealthy. You are allowed to be free.

It starts here. It starts now. It starts with you.

50 Questions

50 thoughtful, practical, and protective questions that dentists can use when interviewing or working with financial professionals, CPAs, estate attorneys, and other key advisors. These questions are designed to help *you* stay in control, ensure alignment, and avoid costly misunderstandings.

Financial Advisors

1. Are you a fiduciary at all times?
2. How do you get paid (fee-only, commission, both)?
3. Do you specialize in working with dentists or healthcare professionals?
4. What financial planning services do you offer beyond investment management?
5. How do you help clients with student loan repayment strategies?
6. Will you help me create a written financial plan?
7. How do you choose investment options for your clients?
8. What's your investment philosophy?
9. How often will we meet or communicate?
10. Can you help me review my disability and life insurance policies?
11. Do you help with practice transition planning or exit strategy?
12. Can you collaborate with my CPA and attorney?
13. How do you manage risk in client portfolios?
14. What benchmarks do you use to evaluate investment performance?
15. How do you approach tax-efficiency in my portfolio?
16. What happens if you retire or leave your firm—who takes over?
17. Can I see a sample client report or dashboard?

18. Have you worked with clients at my stage of career/life?
19. What credentials or certifications do you hold?
20. Can you provide references from other dental clients?

CPAs and Tax Professionals

1. Do you specialize in dental practices or healthcare providers?
2. Can you help with tax planning throughout the year—not just at tax time?
3. How do you help reduce my tax liability legally and ethically?
4. Can you help structure my practice for tax efficiency (S-corp, LLC, etc.)?
5. Do you provide guidance on estimated tax payments?
6. Can you help me understand how to maximize retirement plan deductions?
7. Will you help me plan for equipment purchases and depreciation?
8. How do you stay current on tax law changes affecting dentists?
9. Can you review my prior tax returns for missed opportunities?
10. Do you offer proactive tax strategies for high-income earners?

Estate Planning Attorneys

1. Do you have experience creating estate plans for dentists or business owners?
2. What documents do I need (will, trust, power of attorney, etc.)?
3. How should I structure my estate plan if I own a practice?
4. Can you help with succession planning for my practice?
5. What happens to my business if I become incapacitated or pass away?
6. Do you offer guidance on charitable giving or legacy planning?
7. How often should my estate plan be reviewed or updated?
8. Can you coordinate with my financial advisor and CPA?
9. Will my estate avoid probate with this plan?
10. How do you charge—flat fee or hourly?

Other Professionals (Business Attorneys, Insurance Advisors, Bankers, etc.)

1. What are the biggest legal or financial risks I should be aware of as a practice owner?
2. Can you review my contracts (lease, associate agreements, vendor contracts)?
3. What type of liability protection do I need as a dentist?
4. Do I need an umbrella insurance policy—and how much coverage is appropriate?
5. Can you help structure a buy-sell agreement with a partner?
6. How should I protect my intellectual property (logo, name, procedures)?
7. What do I need to know about hiring/firing from a legal standpoint?
8. Can you help me secure business or equipment loans at competitive rates?
9. Do you work with other dentists or healthcare businesses?
10. How can you help me avoid common legal/financial mistakes in private practice?

Disclaimer

Educational Purpose and Disclaimer

This book, *Financial Literacy For Dentists,* was written with the intent to **educate, empower, and encourage dentists**—whether early in their careers or decades into practice—to take control of their financial lives. The content presented throughout these pages is grounded in the author's personal experience, professional expertise, and extensive research compiled over more than two decades of work in financial services, practice development, and financial education for healthcare professionals.

However, it is critically important to understand the following:

This Is Not Legal, Financial, Investment, Accounting, or Tax Advice

The information provided in this book is for **general educational and informational purposes only**. It should not be relied upon as a substitute for personalized financial, legal, tax, or investment advice from qualified professionals.

Every dentist's situation is unique—based on your income, business structure, debt load, family responsibilities, goals, risk tolerance, and geographic location. What may be appropriate for one dentist may not be safe, beneficial, or suitable for another.

Before making any major financial decisions—including but not limited to investing, purchasing insurance, taking out loans, buying or selling a practice, entering into contracts, or making estate planning decisions—

it is strongly advised that you consult with the appropriate licensed professionals.

No Legal Advice

While some topics discussed in this book may involve legal issues (such as business ownership, estate planning, or employee agreements), this publication does **not provide legal advice** and should not be interpreted as such.

If you are considering:\n

- Creating or modifying contracts,\n
- Structuring a practice partnership or buy-sell agreement,\n
- Drafting wills or trusts,\n
- Handling legal disputes, or\n
- Navigating liability concerns,\n

You should seek guidance from a qualified attorney—preferably one with experience in healthcare law, business law, or estate planning for professionals.

Laws vary significantly by state and jurisdiction, and they are subject to change. You are responsible for staying in compliance with all local, state, and federal regulations that apply to your personal and professional life.

No Investment or Financial Advice

Although this book covers core financial topics—such as budgeting, debt management, saving, retirement planning, insurance, investing, and building wealth—it does so strictly from an **educational standpoint**.

It is not intended to recommend specific investment products, asset allocations, or financial strategies. Financial planning decisions should always be based on your full financial picture, and ideally created in collaboration with a licensed, fiduciary financial advisor who understands the nuances of working with dentists and practice owners.

Never make investment decisions based solely on what you read in any book—this one included—without first seeking advice from a certified financial planner, CPA, or other licensed financial professional.

The author makes no representation or warranty that any of the strategies or ideas shared will result in specific outcomes or guarantees of success.

No Tax or Accounting Advice

This book is not authored by a CPA, tax attorney, or enrolled agent. While it references general tax concepts, including deductions, write-offs, and tax strategies commonly used by dental professionals, **none of this content should be interpreted as tax advice**.

Tax laws are complex, subject to change, and highly individualized based on income level, business structure, investments, and location. If you are seeking tax planning guidance, you should consult a qualified tax professional who understands the healthcare industry and can provide you with a personalized strategy.

Only a licensed CPA or tax advisor can help you:\n

- Properly structure your practice income\n
- Navigate IRS compliance\n
- Plan for estimated taxes or quarterly filings\n
- Reduce tax liabilities legally and ethically\n
- Avoid audit risks or penalties

No Guarantees or Promises

Reading *Financial Literacy For Dentists* does **not guarantee financial success**. This book is intended to help you build awareness, develop confidence, and make informed decisions—but outcomes depend on many factors, including your own behavior, the quality of your professional team, external market conditions, and personal circumstances.

Any case studies, examples, or hypothetical scenarios presented are for illustration purposes only. They are not promises or predictions of your specific results.

Limitation of Liability

By reading this book, you acknowledge that the author, Patrick Brown, MBA, and affiliated platforms—such as FinancialLiteracyForDentists.com—are not responsible for any decisions you make or outcomes you experience as a result of applying the information provided here.

Neither the author nor any associated entity will be liable for any financial loss, legal dispute, tax penalty, or other consequences that may result from your use of the content. You are responsible for conducting your own due diligence and seeking professional advice as needed.

Encouragement to Seek Professional Help

Dentists—especially those who are practice owners—carry a unique and complex set of financial responsibilities. You deserve access to a team of trustworthy professionals, including a fiduciary financial advisor, a healthcare-savvy CPA, and an experienced attorney.

This book is not a substitute for that team—it is designed to **complement** it.

If you do not currently have the right professionals in your corner, this book strongly encourages you to start building that team today. Early, educated decisions have long-lasting effects—on your wealth, your family, your career, and your peace of mind.

You are not alone on this journey.

You are capable of building a financially healthy life and practice—and doing it with clarity, confidence, and purpose.

Dental Financial Planning Calendar

January

Jan 1 – New Tax Year Begins

- Start tracking all practice-related income and expenses using a spreadsheet, Google Sheet, or software like **QuickBooks**, **Xero**, or **Expensify**.
- **Rule of Thumb:** Set aside **25%–35%** of net income for taxes (more if you're self-employed without withholdings).
- **Tip:** Keep a **separate business checking account** just for practice expenses and income.

Jan 15 – 4th Quarter Estimated Tax Payment Due

- If you're a practice owner or self-employed associate and earned significant income without sufficient withholding last year, your 4th quarter estimated taxes are due.
- **Form to Know:** IRS **Form 1040-ES**

Jan 31 – Deadline for Receiving Tax Forms

- Expect to receive:
- **Form 1099-NEC** if you're an independent contractor (associate dentist or consultant)
- **Form 1099-K** for third-party payments via Stripe, PayPal, or Square

(over $600)

- **W-2** from your employer if you're on payroll
- **Tip:** Save all tax forms in a secure digital folder: **"2024 Taxes – Dentistry"**

February

Start Preparing Your Tax Documents

- Gather income statements, receipts, supply orders, CE expenses, travel logs, insurance premiums, and practice-related software subscriptions.
- Track vehicle mileage if you use your car for CE events, mobile dentistry, or supply runs.

Tax Forms to Understand:

- **Schedule C (Form 1040):** Reports self-employed dental income
- **Schedule SE:** Calculates your self-employment taxes (15.3%)

March

March 15 – Tax Filing Deadline for LLCs or S-Corps

- If you elected **S-Corp** status for your dental practice, your corporate return is due.
- **Form to Know: Form 1120S** (S-Corp)
- **Action Step:** Work with your CPA to ensure owner compensation is structured appropriately to optimize taxes.

April

April 15 – Major Tax Deadline

- File your personal **federal income tax return**
- Make your **1st quarter estimated tax payment** for the current year
- Last day to contribute to your **IRA or HSA** for the previous tax year
- **Forms to Know:**
- **Form 1040** (individual return)
- **Form 4868** (extension request)

Tip: File your return even if you can't pay in full—penalties are much worse for failing to file than failing to pay.

June

June 15 – 2nd Quarter Estimated Tax Payment Due

- Especially important for **self-employed dentists**, practice owners, and those earning pass-through income.
- **Mid-Year Tip:** If your income is rising, meet with your CPA now to adjust quarterly tax projections and avoid underpayment penalties.

July

July 1 – Mid-Year Financial Review

- Reassess your personal and business finances:
- Are you on track with savings?
- Are your tax withholdings sufficient?
- Do your current insurance policies (disability, life, malpractice) need updating?
- **Pro Tip:** Review your fee schedule, collections, and overhead ratio

with your practice consultant or CPA.

September

September 15 – 3rd Quarter Estimated Tax Payment Due

- Continue setting aside **25%–35%** of your income if you're a 1099 earner or practice owner.
- **Tax Prep Tip:** Start organizing receipts, mileage logs, and quarterly reports in advance of year-end.

October

October 15 – Final Deadline for Extended Tax Returns

- If you filed for an extension in April, this is your last chance to file your federal tax return.
- **Reminder:** Penalties still apply if you owe and don't pay by April, even if you extended.

November

Begin Year-End Tax Planning

- Schedule a meeting with your **CPA or financial advisor**.
- Review your **Section 179** deductions for equipment purchases.
- Consider prepaying 2025 expenses (marketing, CE, software) to lower 2024 taxable income.
- **Action Step:** Evaluate charitable contributions and donor-advised funds if you itemize.

December

December 31 – Final Day for Many Tax Moves

- Final day to:
- Buy dental equipment for this tax year
- Make charitable donations
- Book CE courses
- Contribute to retirement accounts (Solo 401(k), SEP IRA)
- **Safe Harbor Rule Reminder:**
- If you pay 100% of last year's tax liability (or 110% if your AGI was over $150,000), you may avoid underpayment penalties.

Bonus: Financial Best Practices for Dentists

- **Save 25%–35% of Net Income for Taxes** (especially if self-employed or running a practice)
- **Separate Business and Personal Finances**
- **Use Cloud-Based Tools** like QuickBooks, MileIQ, or Keeper Tax to track expenses
- **Automate Contributions** to IRAs, emergency funds, and investment accounts
- **Meet Quarterly with Your CPA or Advisor** to stay on track
- **Review State and Local Tax Rules** (especially if you own property or employ staff)
- **Document Everything** – mileage, CE expenses, office meals, conferences, marketing campaigns

Final Word

This Book Exists Because Financial Education Is Power

This book exists because financial education is power. It can open doors, protect your legacy, and give you the confidence to take control of your future—not just for your practice, but for your family, your retirement, and your peace of mind.

Financial literacy isn't about becoming a financial expert overnight. It's about developing the awareness to ask better questions, the insight to make more informed choices, and the confidence to take strategic action—on your terms.

Just like dentistry, financial success requires skill, precision, and repetition. And just like in your clinical work, it helps to have a team. Strategy matters. So does discipline. And so does knowing when to call in the right professionals to help you make smart decisions.

Let this book be a guide—not a rule book. Use it as a conversation starter with your CPA, your financial advisor, your attorney. Highlight the parts that resonate. Revisit the sections that challenge you. Most importantly, let it inspire action—not just awareness.

Need Help? Start Here

If you're looking for support in applying what you've learned, or want a partner in your financial journey, start here:

Visit: www.FinancialLiteracyForDentists.com

Email: info@financialliteracyfordentists.com

You'll find tools, updates, and connections designed specifically for dentists. Join the newsletter to stay up to date with new strategies, tax changes, practice ownership insights, and resources you can actually use.

Final Word: Use This—Don't Shelf It

This book was not meant to sit untouched on a shelf.

It was written to help you think, reflect, act, and grow. Whether you're just starting out, running a thriving practice, or preparing for retirement, the principles inside are designed to meet you where you are—and help you move forward with clarity and purpose.

Revisit the chapters. Share them with your spouse, business partners, or team. Mark up the pages. Come back when you're preparing to buy into a practice, review an insurance policy, or wonder if you're saving enough.

Because financial peace doesn't happen all at once. It happens through small, smart, repeated steps—taken consistently over time.

50 Financial Literacy Terms for Dentists

1. **Asset** – Anything you own that has value (cash, equipment, property).
2. **Liability** – Money you owe (loans, credit cards, mortgages).
3. **Net Worth** – Your total assets minus your total liabilities.
4. **Cash Flow** – The money moving in and out of your practice or personal finances.
5. **Profit** – What remains after subtracting expenses from income.
6. **Gross Income** – Income before taxes or expenses are deducted.
7. **Net Income** – Income left after taxes and operating costs.
8. **Budget** – A plan for how you spend and save your money.
9. **Emergency Fund** – Cash reserved for unexpected expenses.
10. **Credit Score** – A number that reflects your creditworthiness.
11. **Debt-to-Income Ratio** – Your total monthly debt payments divided by your income.
12. **Compound Interest** – Earning interest on your principal and the interest already earned.
13. **Diversification** – Spreading money across investments to reduce risk.
14. **Investment Portfolio** – A collection of assets like stocks, bonds, and funds.
15. **Roth IRA** – A retirement account where growth and withdrawals are tax-free (if rules are met).
16. **Traditional IRA** – A retirement account with tax-deferred growth.
17. **401(k)** – An employer-sponsored retirement plan, often with matching contributions.
18. **SEP IRA** – A retirement account for self-employed or small business

owners.

19. **Solo 401(k)** – A retirement plan for business owners with no employees.
20. **Brokerage Account** – An investment account to buy and sell securities.
21. **ETF (Exchange-Traded Fund)** – A bundle of stocks or bonds traded like a stock.
22. **Mutual Fund** – A pooled investment managed by professionals.
23. **Capital Gain** – Profit made from selling an asset at a higher price than purchase.
24. **Depreciation** – The loss of value over time, often used for tax deductions.
25. **Write-Off** – A business expense that reduces taxable income.
26. **Tax Deduction** – A reduction in taxable income based on certain expenses.
27. **Form 1099** – IRS form reporting income from work outside traditional employment.
28. **Schedule C** – Tax form for reporting income and expenses as a sole proprietor.
29. **Estimated Taxes** – Quarterly tax payments for self-employed or high-income earners.
30. **Audit** – A review of your tax records by the IRS or tax authority.
31. **Liability Insurance** – Protects your practice if someone is injured or sues.
32. **Malpractice Insurance** – A must-have for healthcare professionals to cover legal claims.
33. **Disability Insurance** – Replaces income if you're unable to work due to illness or injury.
34. **Term Life Insurance** – Life insurance that provides coverage for a set period.
35. **Whole Life Insurance** – Permanent coverage that builds cash value over time.
36. **Operating Expenses** – Day-to-day costs to run your practice.

37. **Accounts Receivable** – Money owed to your practice by patients or insurers.
38. **Accounts Payable** – Bills and obligations your practice owes to others.
39. **Practice Valuation** – Estimating the worth of your dental business.
40. **Equity** – Ownership interest in a business or asset.
41. **Loan Amortization** – Paying off a loan with regular payments over time.
42. **Overhead** – Fixed and variable expenses needed to operate your practice.
43. **Practice Management Software** – Tools for scheduling, billing, and records.
44. **Revenue Cycle Management** – The process of billing, collecting, and processing income.
45. **Break-Even Point** – When revenue equals expenses (no profit, no loss).
46. **Succession Planning** – Preparing for the transfer of practice ownership.
47. **Estate Planning** – Arranging for the transfer of your assets after death.
48. **Trust** – A legal entity to manage assets for future use or beneficiaries.
49. **Power of Attorney** – A legal document allowing someone to act on your behalf financially or medically.
50. **Financial Planner** – A professional who helps manage money, investments, taxes, and goals.

About the Author

Pat Brown, MBA

Pat Brown, MBA, is a seasoned financial advisor, educator, and advocate for professionals navigating complex financial landscapes—including dentists, doctors, and business owners. With over two decades of experience in wealth management, insurance strategy, and financial education, Pat brings a rare combination of real-world expertise, relatable storytelling, and a deep passion for helping others build financial stability and long-term wealth.

Raised in a household where money conversations were rare and financial literacy was not taught, Pat knows firsthand the consequences of financial unawareness—and the life-changing power of understanding your money. That personal journey fuels his mission today: to make financial literacy approachable, relevant, and empowering for high-earning professionals, especially those in demanding careers like dentistry.

After earning his MBA and working as a trusted wealth advisor, Pat began to recognize a troubling pattern—dentists often leave dental school buried in debt, with little to no training in managing their finances, building a business, or protecting their assets. He created *FinancialLiteracyForDentists.com* to bridge that gap and equip dental professionals with the tools they need to thrive both chairside and beyond.

Through his national speaking engagements, workshops, and online platforms, Pat has educated thousands on key topics like budgeting, credit, investing, tax planning, insurance, practice ownership, and generational wealth. His teaching style is grounded in practicality, humility, and a genuine desire to help others make confident, informed decisions.

More than a financial expert, Pat is a mentor, husband, and father who believes that financial freedom isn't just about numbers—it's about designing a life of purpose, security, and peace. His work is built on the belief that financial literacy isn't a luxury for dentists—it's a necessity.

Made in United States
Orlando, FL
04 November 2026

90201055R00213